SHARING JESUS WITH MUSLIMS IN AMERICA

Abu Daoud

Northumberland Historical Press

Northumberland Historical Press
PO Box 460
Heathsville, VA 22473

Copyright © 2016 by Abu Daoud
All rights reserved.

Unless otherwise noted, Scripture quotations are from the
New Revised Standard Version.

ISBN-13: 978-1539013259
ISBN-10: 1539013251
Library of Congress Control Number: 2016950479

Printed in the United States of America

CONTENTS

INTRODUCTION   1

1. THE NEED   5

    A Call From Within   7
    A Call From Without   9
    A Call From Below   13
    A Call from Above   15
    Summary   16

2. THE VANTAGE   19

    Historical Background   19
    Population Trends   26
    Why People are Leaving
        Muhammad for Jesus   33
    The Scriptural Vantage   43
    Summary   46

3. THE WITNESS: ONE BELIEVER   47

    The Right Philosophy for
        Witnessing to Muslims   49
    Key Elements for Muslim Ministry   58
    Suggestions for Meeting and
        Working with Muslims   63

Ways to Get a Religious
    Conversation Started   66
Summary   73

4. CHURCH MOBILIZATION   75

Know Your Muslim Neighbor   77
English as a Foreign Language   81
International Student Meals   83
Refugee Settlement   87
Muslim-Christian Discussion Groups   89
The Internet   91
Summary   92

5. THE KNOWLEDGE   95

Some of Your Muslim Friend's Beliefs   96
An Analogy from India   100
Introducing the Major Topics   102
   Holy Scripture   103
   God and Allah   108
   Sin   111
   The Person of Jesus, the Son of God   120
   The Tri-Unity of God, the Trinity   123
   The Cross and the Atonement   128
   One Gospel   136
Summary   139

6. THE TRUE RELIGION   141

Leadership Structure   144
Mission Statement   144
Method for Growth   146

Code of Conduct 146
Rituals 147
Summary 147

CONCLUSION 151

...53

...out the Holy Bible 153
...he Qur'an 154
...he Bible
...Islam 155
...out Jesus 157
...Verses 159
...rses 161

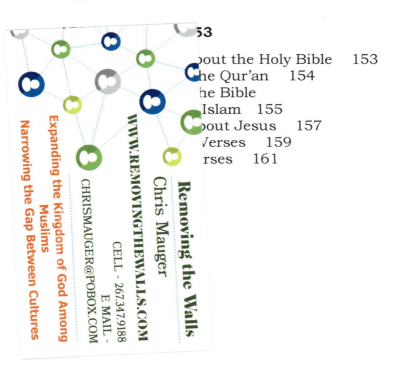

INTRODUCTION

Passion!

You see the crowd of passionate men protesting against the drone strikes in Pakistan or against a magazine that published cartoons of Muhammad. There is no question that they are full of passion.

You see the woman wearing the face covering, and question why she is here. Why doesn't she go back to wherever she is from or at least dress like the rest of us? The man with the beard and the robe on TV who wants to open a big new mosque in your city: Why is he here? If he likes Islam so much, why doesn't he go live in a Muslim-majority country? Or what about young Muslim men and women stating clearly that they are Americans and want Shari'a law in this country, too?

What are Christians to make of the rapidly growing number of Muslims in the United States? But the more important question is: How does God want his church to respond? In this book, I argue that American Christians are living in a time of opportunity according to God's providence, and they must respond to their new Muslim neighbors by sharing the gospel with them.

The more you and I allow the Spirit of God to direct our thoughts, the more passionate we become. However, the passion that grows within us is not to conquer or destroy a perceived enemy. No! It is a passion to become compassionate. God is passionate about people worshiping him in spirit and truth, and we should be passionate for the same thing.

This book is written from the blood, sweat, and tears of experience. I lived for many years in foreign countries where Islam plays a key role in daily life. I grew in my passion to see Muslims as God sees them. This passion has grown so strong that I want you to join me in working to grow the kingdom of God among the Muslim people of your area. I am writing to those of you who want to share the love of God with your Muslim neighbors.

As the book title suggests, I believe God is bringing Muslims to America so they can hear and accept the gospel. It is not my desire to see this group of people as traditional American Christians, giving up their cultural heritage. Instead, I want to reflect God's passion and welcome Muslims into the rich cultural mosaic of the kingdom of God. In God's plan, I believe that Muslims are coming to America so that Christians can show them true passion and true joy.

This book is going to help you share the gospel with Muslims. The chapters are as follows:

Chapter 1. The Need: Why Christians need to address the issue of Muslims in the United States.

Chapter 2. The Vantage: How Christians should view Muslims in the United States.

Chapter 3. The Witness, One Believer: How an individual with the intent of sharing the gospel can meet Muslims.

Chapter 4. Church Mobilization: How a congregation or group within a church might reach out to local Muslims.

Chapter 5. The Knowledge: Basic information that people should know about Islam and interacting with Muslims.

Chapter 6. The True Religion: How the Christian faith meets the deepest needs of the human soul.

I intend for this book to be practical and easy to read. I want you to know that currently many Muslims are accepting the gospel message and entering the kingdom of God. That is my passion, and I hope it will become yours too.

I opened the introduction with a description of passionate Muslims in the street crying out for a cause. Now picture the same group of people worshiping the God and Father of our Lord Jesus

Christ with the same passion. It can happen, but it will take all of us sharing our passion for God with our Muslim neighbors.

Chapter 1

THE NEED

When was the first time you became aware of Muslims living in your country? In your neighborhood? Initially, most Muslims lived in major cities or near large universities. Now they live in almost every neighborhood in America. Some are working as laborers while others are doctors, executives, and entrepreneurs.

I believe the influx of Muslims into America can lead to some wonderful results. This is a special season in God's sovereign plan. Most missionaries do a wonderful job and their work is vital to the kingdom of God. However, I know from firsthand experience that living and ministering in Muslim-dominated countries is often difficult. The work is not easy, can be dangerous sometimes, and often requires a great deal of resources and perseverance to maintain. But contrast this with Muslims moving to your neighborhood: The task of sharing the gospel becomes much easier.

This chapter focuses on why Christians need to address the issue of Muslims in America. We will address this topic from four points of view, loosely based on a sermon by the Rev. Mark Finley.[1] Finley states that there are four calls for evangelism: from within, from without, from below, and from above. With this sermon as a starting point, we'll explore how Finley's four calls fit into the church's mission to Muslims.

God desires his people to be on a mission. The children of Israel were instructed to first teach future generations the stories of God's deliverance and guidance (Exodus 12:24-27, Deuteronomy 6:4-9, Isaiah 38:19). Secondly, their mission activity was directed toward people who were not of faith.[2] In the New Testament, the disciples and every follower of Jesus are commanded to make disciples, baptizing them in the name of the Father, Son and Holy Spirit.[3] Making disciples among your Muslim neighbors is part of that mission—an urgent part.

There are several very good reasons why Christians need to address the issue of Muslims in America. The opposite is either ignoring or resisting the fact that Muslims are in our

---

[1] Mark Finley, "God's Four Calls for Evangelism," last modified September 16, 2015. Used by permission. (https://www.youtube.com/watch?v=D6JhHuK-pq0). Outline and selected details used with permission.
[2] 1 Kings 8:41
[3] Matthew 28:19

neighborhoods, an ungodly response. Let's explore some of these reasons.

Finley uses four different passages from the Bible to emphasize the reasons why each follower of Jesus should be active in evangelism. These four calls clearly apply to Muslims, just as they apply to the entire world.

A CALL FROM WITHIN

The first call to evangelism is a call from within, as explained in Romans 1:14-16:

> I am a debtor both to Greeks and to barbarians, both to the wise and to the foolish—hence my eagerness to proclaim the gospel to you also who are in Rome. For I am not ashamed of the gospel; it is the power of God for salvation to everyone who has faith, to the Jew first and also to the Greek.

Committed evangelists will find a way to share their faith no matter what the situation or location. The Apostle Paul was one of the people who understood that the gospel is most important. To him and many others, the gospel is like a burning story that must get out. There is a story recorded in Acts 3-4 that illustrates this point.

Peter and John were on their way to the temple to pray when a beggar asked them for money. Peter told the man he had no money and promptly healed him. A crowd gathered, so Peter preached to the crowd, and five thousand people believed the gospel message. This angered the religious leaders so they had Peter and John arrested. The main point of contention was that Peter and John preached Jesus, resurrected from the dead. Once again, during the questioning, Peter declared the gospel to his captors. After their release, Peter and John rejoiced with follow believers.

In this story, the two men continually shared the gospel. The event started when they crossed a cultural barrier, interacting with a beggar. The beggar was probably dirty, smelly, and ignored by most of the people walking past. It was likely that even those who gave him money laid it near him for fear of touching him. However, Peter and John saw the beggar as a person created in God's image. Even before the healing took place, they had assigned value to this man who slept in the dirt. After the healing, Peter and John used the attention the healing received to share the gospel. Not only did they share with the crowd with great results, but they also shared with the religious leaders.

Satan is against a call from within. He wants believers to be self-centered and resist the urge God gives us to share the gospel. One of the ways he does this is by promoting a we-versus-they mentality. When Christians erect barriers that prevent Muslims from hearing or experiencing the gospel, Satan wins. Just as physical walls require regular maintenance, psychological walls of prejudice, distrust, and hate must be maintained at the expense of the relationships they sever and the peace they forfeit.

Please do not allow Satan to have this victory! Guard your minds and your hearts. Remember, the gospel is for all people: rich, poor, white, black, Jew, Gentile, and Muslim. Therefore, let us check our hearts and minds. Do we have a burning desire to share the gospel? Are we willing to share it with everyone we meet? Finally, are we willing to take this message to the Muslims in our area? Christians need to address the issue of Muslims in America because there is a God-given desire from within to share the good news of Jesus with all people. In later chapters, I will address the question of how, but first we must be willing. As stated by Finely, "A soul winner always has soul winning on his or her mind."

A CALL FROM WITHOUT

The second call to evangelism is from without, as suggested by Luke 19:10, which states, "For the Son of Man has come to seek and to save that which was lost."

While Jesus was on the earth, he attracted a large crowd wherever he went. Some thought he would become a political leader, and others flocked to him hoping he would heal their physical diseases. One of the remarkable truths about Jesus was that he took time to care for the people who came to him. He looked people in the eye, he touched them, and he spent time with them. He never said he was too busy or too important to deal with people. He was about his Father's business.[4]

Jesus looked on both the outside and inside of the people he met. He knew what people were thinking even though they did not always speak.[5] Have you ever considered what it would be like to see people as Jesus did? Perhaps we do not always want to know what another is thinking, but what if we were to see others with the compassion of Jesus? At one point, Jesus looked over Jerusalem and said:

Jerusalem, Jerusalem, the city that kills the prophets and stones those who are sent to it! How often have I desired to gather your children together as a hen gathers her brood under her wings, and you were not willing!"[6]

The call from without is a call of compassion. It is looking at a nation, a city, a neighborhood, a family, and a person with the eyes of Jesus. A call

---

[4] Luke 2:49, John 4:34
[5] Matthew 12:25
[6] Matthew 23:37

The Need 11

from without is to see these groups and conclude that each of them needs the gospel message. The gospel is for those in need, and we are all in need, including the Muslims. The gospel is meant to be both preached and lived out. A wonderful example of a healthy relationship between faith and works is found in the book of James.[7] In that book, James makes the point that a statement of faith and one's actions work in tandem to show the true nature of a person's relationship with God.

A Bible professor repeatedly asked a question during his classes: "Is the church a hotel for saints or a hospital for sinners?" Let us compare the two and then make several points of application.

First the hotel. A hotel is all about keeping the guests comfortable. Every day, the rooms are cleaned and fresh towels provided. Food is available at all times and one or more taxi services stand ready to whisk people to their desired destinations. The guests have no other job than to be guests (and pay the bill). The job of the staff is to keep the guests happy at all times.

Second, let us consider the hospital. A hospital is a special place where the sick become well. Doctors and nurses are prepared to handle every type of case that comes their way. The hospital

---

[7]James 2:19ff

stores medical supplies and equipment, all of which are ready at a moment's notice. When the ambulance arrives with an emergency patient, skilled professionals come running, ready to do whatever it takes to save a life. A hospital serves its community in a much different way than does a hotel.

Hotels and hospitals serve specific but differing purposes, and no one confuses the two. When you and I consider the condition of today's world, a hospital seems like a more fitting image of what a church should be. Apparently, this was also true in Jesus' day. When the Bible states that Jesus was about his Father's business, it meant that he was busy restoring people. Our world is full of hurting people who need a church to act as a hospital does, healing their hurt with the grace of God rather than pampering them and catering to their whims as a hotel does.

One of the ways to fulfill the second call of evangelism is to do ministry as if it were a life and death profession. The life in our hands is that of the patient, the Muslim who will die eternally without your intervention. There is an urgent need for people to pour out compassion on the Muslims of the world. It is time to convert hotel-type churches into ones that focus on the sick and dying.

A CALL FROM BELOW

The third call of evangelism is a call from below, found in the following passage. Although Finley references Hebrews 11:39-40 in his sermon, I think Luke 16:19-31 is appropriate for this discussion:

> There was a rich man who was dressed in purple and fine linen and who feasted sumptuously every day. And at his gate lay a poor man named Lazarus, covered with sores, who longed to satisfy his hunger with what fell from the rich man's table; even the dogs would come and lick his sores. The poor man died and was carried away by the angels to be with Abraham. The rich man also died and was buried. In Hades, where he was being tormented, he looked up and saw Abraham far away with Lazarus by his side. He called out, "Father Abraham, have mercy on me, and send Lazarus to dip the tip of his finger in water and cool my tongue; for I am in agony in these flames." But Abraham said, "Child, remember that during your lifetime you received your good things, and Lazarus in like manner evil things; but now he is comforted here, and you are in agony. Besides all this, between you and us a great chasm has been fixed, so that those who might want to pass from here to you cannot do so, and no one can cross from there to us." He said, "Then, father, I beg you to send him to my father's house—for I have five brothers—that he may warn them, so that they will not also come into this place of

torment." Abraham replied, "They have Moses and the prophets; they should listen to them." He said, "No, father Abraham; but if someone goes to them from the dead, they will repent." He said to him, "If they do not listen to Moses and the prophets, neither will they be convinced even if someone rises from the dead."

It is very sad to think about the people who have gone to hell because they rejected God's gift of eternal life in Jesus Christ during their earthly lifetimes. Regardless of how we interpret the image of hell in this parable, it is clear that no one in hell wants to be there. Modern society often suggests that hell is not a real place or, if it is, God would not send anyone there. This is a lie from Satan that in no way is supported by the Bible. In this parable, the rich man is so desperate that he asks for a drop of water (implying he does not have any water) and when he cannot have that, he begs that a message be sent to his family members. Notice also that neither he nor Abraham is able to move between the two places.

We do not believe anything has changed since the time Jesus told this story. No one on earth can comprehend the beauty of heaven and the repulsiveness of hell. However, people in hell still want their friends and family to do whatever it takes to avoid the place. Have you ever considered that there are Muslims in hell wishing we would reach out to their family members?

In response, Satan says hell is not real; all religions lead to heaven. He tells us that if we are in faith, no one else matters or those people are not worth it. These days Satan is influencing some people to focus on nationalism and ignore the reality of what happens when someone does not accept Jesus as Savior. When the cares of an earthly nation supersede the gospel message, there is a serious problem. No nation is more important than the kingdom of God. Nations will rise and fall but the Word of God will remain forever.

The cry from hell is, "Keep my family members out of this place." Let us listen to this cry and do what we can to make sure Muslims accept the gospel of Jesus, the Messiah.

A CALL FROM ABOVE

Finally, the fourth call of evangelism is a call from above, found in Luke 15. That chapter features three stories of something lost and then found. Verse 7 summarizes the chapter, "Just so, I tell you, there will be more joy in heaven over one sinner who repents than over ninety-nine righteous persons who need no repentance." Think of it this way: Soul winning brings joy to heaven and to God himself.

Right before he returned to heaven, Jesus told his disciples to go and make disciples. Then in the book of Acts, we read how the church grew because the disciples obeyed his command. This trend has not changed at all. Throughout history, true followers of Jesus shared the gospel and the kingdom of God grew. And as the kingdom grew, heaven rejoiced.

Satan does not want the kingdom of God to grow. He tries to convince us that the task is impossible or too dangerous. He also tries to shift our focus away from God's glory to ourselves. Finally, he wants us to believe that our efforts are futile and better off left undone. Each one of these thoughts is untrue and should be rejected immediately. God has given us both the privilege and the responsibility to share the gospel with Muslims around the world.

SUMMARY

This chapter uses Mark Finley's sermon, "The Four Calls to Evangelism," as its basic outline. The calls are: (1) from within, (2) from without, (3) from below, and (4) from above. The text presents each of these calls in light of a Bible reference, an illustration, and an example of how Satan works in direct opposition to the calls.

God calls us to reach out to all people. This book is about how you can and should reach out to Muslims. The job is not impossible, especially when one works with God's power. Jesus said, "The harvest is plentiful but the workers are few."[8] Those words are just as true today as when Jesus said them two thousand years ago. It is time to fill the gap. It is time to step up and get involved. God does not want people spending eternity separated from him. As we make the kingdom of God our first priority, these four calls will become a reality in our daily lives.

Let us join the heavenly host, rejoicing as Muslim people enter God's kingdom. With this in mind, let us move to the next chapter, learning more about the growing presence of Muslims in the West and the United States in particular.

---

[8] Matthew 9:37-38

Chapter 2
THE VANTAGE

Some years ago there was a video on YouTube that talked about Europe's Islamic future. It frightened many people, but ultimately many of the numbers in that video were revealed as dubious if not outright wrong. So let us take a more rational look at the migration of Muslims to the West in the coming decades. The goal of this chapter is to share an adequate and informed vantage point from which to understand the nature and magnitude of Islam in the West.

Before I start, though, I want to be clear in explaining my goal: It is *not* to stir up fear or hatred. Quite the opposite and this view will be reiterated many times throughout the book: My goal is to encourage Christians to reach out in love to their Muslim neighbors.

HISTORICAL BACKGROUND

Have you ever heard that Christianity has spread westward, age by age? According to this story, it originated in Palestine, spread into the Roman

Empire and then to the Americas, before coming full circle in the twentieth century as Christianity quickly grew in the East. This story is completely and totally false. Christianity at first spread westward *and* eastward into what are now Iran and China and parts of India, but the churches in those regions largely declined or became extinct later on. One of the main reasons (but not the only one) that Christianity declined and in some places vanished, was Islam.

Have you ever heard the saying, "The blood of the martyrs is the seed of the church"? That quote goes back to the great North African church father of the third century, Tertullian of Carthage. Carthage was once a thriving church and today it is a neighborhood in the Tunisian capital city of Tunis, which is less than one percent Christian. Maybe we need to modify that phrase to, "The blood of the martyrs is the seed of the church, except when Islam is involved." Certainly in some cases, that would be more accurate.

There have been great churches that are now completely dead, even churches that produced artists and missionaries and theologians and mystics. I mention these realities because it is important for Christians to abandon any sense of triumphalism. The victory of Christ over all the powers of the world is both historically and eschatologically accomplished. This is a spiritual victory, which has had and will have physical results. However, prior to Jesus' second coming, there will remain a battle between light and dark, good and evil, righteousness and sin. At various times and in some locations, the kingdom of God seems to be advancing while at other times and places the kingdom of Satan seems to be advancing.

The twentieth century is often viewed as the great century of Christian missionary work, and surely there were successes in some places: the growth of Pentecostalism in Latin America, the rapid expansion of Christianity of all types in sub-Saharan Africa, the growth and maturation of Protestantism in South Korea, and the maturation of Chinese Christianity. But the twentieth century is really a mixed bag, and for every instance of church growth, one can point to great defeats, such as the near elimination of Christianity in much of the Middle East (its birth place!); the decline of the once great Protestant churches of Europe and North America (Episcopal, Anglican, Presbyterian, Methodist, Lutheran) and their increasing irrelevance in relation to global missions; and the eradication of Christianity in another ancient homeland of Anatolia (Turkey).

And during this century of missions, what happened with Islam? I don't want to go into a long chapter on the history of Christian missions to the

Muslim world here (though if I did it would be worth our time), but let me make a few points about the failure of the Church to evangelize Muslims.

1) There were missions to Christians in Muslim lands. We can point to missionary work in the Muslim world, and indeed when I lived in the Middle East, the churches we attended were the fruit of such labor. Scores of missionaries left the United States and Germany and England in order to go to the Ottoman Empire and share the gospel with Christians (and sometimes Jews). Very rarely does one hear about a convert from Islam. We should be sympathetic, though, since both the Muslims who converted and the Christians who encouraged them to convert were subject to great danger. But, with the exception of a couple of brilliant figures (Sam Zwemer and Temple Gairdner being the best known), the bulk of missionary work in the Ottoman Empire and other Muslim lands was not focused on evangelizing Muslims. Getting Christians from the ancient churches there (Orthodox, Maronite, etc.) to become *Protestant* Christians was a priority, and educating and giving medical treatment to Muslims was important. But actually converting Muslims to Christianity was dangerous and, though sundry missionary publications paid lip

The Vantage 23

service to Muslim conversions, they rarely occurred.

2) The great sources of converts in the twentieth century were animists or folk religionists. Have you noticed how little progress the gospel made in North Africa in the twentieth century? That is because the region had been thoroughly Islamized for centuries. The great instances of progress were in regions such as sub-Saharan Africa, which was largely animist, and in China, which was largely a peculiar mélange of Communist atheism and traditional folk religion. In other words, there were no great leaps forward in any Muslim lands, with Indonesia being a possible exception. Throughout its history, Islam has proved to be highly resistant to the Christian message.

3) Something curious happened in the second half of the twentieth century, though. Suddenly, substantial numbers of Muslims converted to Christianity. The number of converts from Islam cannot compare to the number from other religions in China or sub-Saharan Africa, but they are real. The first wave occurred in Indonesia in the 1960s and 1970s; then other movements took root in Iran and among Diaspora Iranians in Algeria, Turkey, Egypt, India, and among some Muslim populations in the West. On a global scale, the numbers are so small that they are of little significance—mere

rounding errors. But historically, these movements really are unique and unprecedented.

Why is this conversion of Muslims to Christianity happening now? There are many factors. Some are religious, like the focus on unreached people groups and the 10/40 window; others are related to globalization and the easy movement of people around the globe; and still others are related to technology and the ease of sharing information via the Internet or satellite television. In any case, let me point out that there is something special about the Christian message that appeals to at least some Muslims, who risk life and limb to follow Jesus and become living members of the community he founded—the Church.

4) We did not go to them, so God is bringing them to us. My evaluation above indicates that Christians did indeed engage in mission among Muslims and in the Muslim world, but actually evangelizing Muslims generally was not a priority. Even when some new missionary had a vision for evangelizing Muslims, such as Horatio Southgate, missionary bishop in Constantinople, the years tended to modify the vision from evangelizing Muslims to... well, anything else. The large influx of Muslims to the West is properly understood in light of the providence of God and because of his desire that all people should hear the gospel. The

church at large did not evangelize Muslims because it was difficult, expensive, and dangerous, but a quick review of the Great Commission reveals no exceptions. Imagine, "Go... and make disciples of all peoples [unless it is dangerous], baptize them in the name of the Father, the Son, and the Holy Spirit, and teach them to obey all that I have commanded you ..."[1]

I am aware that the influx of Muslims has produced a number of difficulties and challenges, including the rise of militant Islam (some people call it extremism—a silly word) among some Muslim youth; the reality that some members of a growing Muslim population quite reasonably want to incorporate parts of the Shari'a into the civil code; and so on. I am not minimizing or ignoring these things, but let me quote Martin Luther on this: "Even the devil is God's devil." As messy as the large-scale immigration of Muslims to the West has been and will continue to be, it has forced the Church to ask the question: What about my Muslim neighbor? And that is a good thing.

Historically, the growth and expansion of Islam has sometimes been linked directly to a lack of unity among Christians, as well as to a failure of the Church to carry out its cross-cultural

---

[1] Matthew 28:19

missionary calling to "make disciples of all peoples."[9] The next time you meet Christians who are disconcerted about the growth of Islam in the West, remind them of some of these historical lessons, and remind them also that this amounts to God forcing the Church to do what it neglected to do for centuries—share the gospel with Muslims.

The reality is that Islam has grown quickly in the West, and every sociological trend (migration, fertility, conversion) indicates that this growth will continue, as discussed in the next section.

POPULATION TRENDS

There has been a significant increase in the migration of Muslims to non-Muslim countries, which gives them much easier access to the Christian message than anything they would have experienced in most of the Muslim world.

Some time ago, a study was done on what happened in the twentieth century when unprecedented numbers of Muslims started converting to Christianity. The question was put to a number of Christian ministers with extensive experience in Muslim communities. "Muslims are experiencing first-hand life in societies in which Christian thought is widespread," wrote one Western minister who had lived in the Middle East and East Africa. One priest indigenous to the

Middle East explicitly tied migration to globalization, answering the question this way: "Globalization and the interaction of cultures due to travel, immigration [to non-Muslim countries], refugees, and international students." Another minister indigenous to the Middle East emphasized the economic causes of emigration, pointing to the increasing "...number of Muslims who departed the region, looking for better conditions of life in the West, where they become, through their daily experience, exposed to Christian values and Christian education."

The overall picture is that once out of the Muslim world, Muslims have a newfound freedom to ask questions and seek answers, including ones about God and his will. This means that Christians, as individuals and as communities, should put their best feet forward—and this will be addressed in the next two chapters.

Let us now search for some hard numbers about Islam in the West. In this section I am intentionally including figures about principal European countries, and not only the United States. My reason for doing this is two-fold: First, there is so much controversy about Islam in Europe that, even for Americans, the topic is an important one. Second, historically and culturally, as much as we might think that Europe and North America are very different from each other, they are different in the way that two brothers are different from each other, and the future of Europe may well offer us some hints about the future of the United States.

It is difficult to find precise figures for how many Muslims migrate to the West. Many countries in the West do not keep a record of the religion of new immigrants. Nor is nationality always a good indicator of religion. Sometimes religious minorities emigrate in larger numbers proportionate to their percentage of the indigenous population of a country. Examples of this are Christians emigrating from Palestine, Lebanon, and Iraq. In the same way, the number of converts from Islam to Christianity is politically sensitive. Some groups overstate the immigration numbers to stir up fear among non-Muslims, or even among Muslims from a different ethnicity. Figures could be overstated also to accrue greater political power to one or another Islamic society or organization. Similarly, the figures might be minimized by a group, either Muslim or non-Muslim. A Muslim organization might want to minimize figures in an effort to stymie the tightening of immigration laws. A non-Muslim political group might want to do the same thing for similar reasons—to show the non-Muslim population that there is no need for immigration reform—thus courting the votes of groups who support such a stance. In sum, gathering precise numbers is no easy task.

However, there are some solid sources of information. One is the respected Pew Forum: "The number of Muslims in Europe has grown from 29.6 million in 1990 to 44.1 million in 2010. Europe's Muslim population is expected to exceed 58 million by 2030."[2] The Pew Forum is generally regarded as reliable, but the figures do not tell us how many of the current Muslim population consists of Muslim immigrants or children of immigrants. Some European Muslim communities, such as those in Albania and Bosnia, have been both European and Muslim for at least two centuries. In this same source, we do have helpful estimates about the number of Muslims immigrating into various European countries, but only for 2010. Without several more years of data for comparison, it is not possible to identify with certainty a trend of increasing Muslim immigration.

One thing that is very clear regarding the West is that the Muslim population is growing as a

---

[2] Pew Forum, 2011, "The Future of the Global Muslim Population," Accessed April 9, 2012 (www.pewforum.org/future-of-the-global-muslim-population-regional-europe.aspx). For some of the charts, see Duane Miller, *Living among the Breakage: Contextual Theology-making and ex-Muslim Christians*, Chapter 3 (Pickwick, 2016). The charts are used with permission.

percentage of the population. The precise relationship of this to immigration is not possible to identify at the moment. This growth is due both to immigration and high Muslim fertility rates. Table 1 shows figures for major European countries from the same Pew Forum report cited above, including projections out to 2030:

Table 1 NUMBER OF MUSLIMS AND PERCENTAGE OF TOTAL POPULATION IN EUROPEAN COUNTRIES					
Country	1990	2000	2010	2020	2030
France	568,000 (1%)	1,401,000 (2.4%)	3,574,000 (5.7%)	4,613,000 (7.1%)	5,620,000 (8.5%)
UK	1,172,000 (2.1%)	1,590,000 (2.7%)	2,869,000 (4.6%)	4,231,000 (6.5%)	5,567,000 (8.2%)
Germany	2,506,000 (3.2%)	3,648,000 (4.5%)	4,119,000 (5.0%)	4,878,000 (6.1%)	5,545,000 (7.1%)
Spain	271,000 (.7%)	419,000 (1.0%)	1,021,000 (2.3%)	1,585,000 (3.3%)	1,859,000 (3.7%)
Sweden	147,000 (1.7%)	226,000 (2.6%)	451,000 (4.9%)	730,000 (7.5%)	993,000 (9.9%)
Italy	858,000 (1.5%)	1,267,000 (2.2%)	1,583,000 (2.6%)	2,425,000 (4.0%)	3,199,000 (5.4%)

Based on the Pew figures, from 1990 through 2030, the Muslim population of France will have increased by 989 percent, the UK by 475 percent, Germany by 221 percent, Spain by 686 percent, Sweden by 675 percent, and Italy by 373 percent. This growth is almost certainly due to both immigration and high birth rates in Muslim families. Note also that these figures are almost certainly low because they were compiled *before* the massive wave of Muslim immigration that started in the summer of 2015.

The same Pew report gave the following figures in Table 2 for Australia, Canada, and the United States:

Table 2 NUMBER OF MUSLIMS AND PERCENTAGE OF TOTAL POPULATION IN AUSTRALIA, CANADA, AND UNITED STATES					
Country	1990	2000	2010	2020	2030
Australia	154,000 (.9%)	290,000 (1.5%)	399,000 (1.9%)	560,000 (2.4%)	714,000 (2.8%)
Canada	313,000 (1.1%)	600,000 (2.0%)	940,000 (2.8%)	1,854,000 (5.0%)	2,661,000 (6.6%)
United States	1,529,000 (.6%)	1,727,000 (.6%)	2,595,000 (.8%)	4,150,000 (1.2%)	6,216,000 (1.7%)

All in all, the Pew report projects that from 1990 to 2030, the Muslim population of Australia will have increased by 463 percent, the United States Muslim population by 406 percent, and the Canadian Muslim population by 850 percent.

I believe that the Pew figures are conservative because they do not take into account new factors leading to emigration. Examples include civil wars in Afghanistan, Iraq, Syria, and Yemen; and the failure of countries—such as Egypt, Pakistan,

Yemen, Somalia, Iraq, and Afghanistan—to provide sufficient food and water for their populations. In addition, while fertility rates are fairly low in some Muslim-majority countries (Iran, Tunisia), in other countries (Yemen, Egypt) the fertility rates are declining slowly while infant mortality declines. Furthermore, if the dire climate change predictions come to pass, then increasing violence over already scarce resources will almost certainly ensue. The result will be an increased number of asylum seekers and refugees, potentially much higher than anything produced by the wars in Iraq or Afghanistan.

Finally, the pace of Muslim migration to the United States is growing substantially:

> In 1992, 41 percent of new permanent residents in the United States—green-card holders—hailed from the Asia-Pacific region, the Middle East and North Africa, or sub-Saharan Africa, according to the Pew Research Center. A decade later, the percentage was 53 percent. Over that same period, predictably, the number of Muslim immigrants coming to the United States annually has doubled, from 50,000 to approximately 100,000 each year. In 1992, only 5 percent of Muslim immigrants came from sub-Saharan Africa; 20 years later, it was 16 percent. Of the 2.75 million Muslims in

the United States in 2011, 1.7 million were legal permanent residents.[3]

In sum, all indicators point to continued migration from Muslim countries to countries with a Christian heritage and some degree of freedom of religion.

But this continued growth of Islam in the West is not the only story in town. Beginning in the 1960s, we started to see an unprecedented movement of people who left Islam for Jesus Christ. In the next section we'll explore why some people have made this move.

WHY PEOPLE ARE LEAVING MUHAMMAD FOR JESUS

Multiple studies exist to explain why people convert from Islam to Christianity. The study we'll be using in this chapter is based on interviews with over four hundred people from thirty-five different countries.[4] The study listed seven of the most popular answers. In order of frequency the reasons

---

[3] Ian Tuttle, "The Troubling Math of Muslim Migration," *National Review* (http://www.nationalreview.com/article/411487/troubling-math-muslim-migration-ian-tuttle), January 13, 2015.

[4] J. Dudley Woodberry, Russell G. Shubin, and G. Mark, "Why Muslims Follow Jesus: The Results of a Recent Survey of Converts from Islam," *Christianity Today*, October 24, 2007, 80.

were: (1) lifestyles of believers, (2) physical healing via prayer in Jesus' name, (3) deliverance from demons via prayer in Jesus' name, (4) dissatisfaction with Islam, (5) dreams and visions, (6) spiritual truth in the Holy Bible, and (7) love of God in the Holy Bible. Let's go through this list one by one and learn more about what attracts people to Jesus Christ, his message, and his community.

Lifestyles of Believers

> But how are they to call on one in whom they have not believed? And how are they to believe in one of whom they have never heard? And how are they to hear without someone to proclaim him? And how are they to proclaim him unless they are sent? As it is written, "How beautiful are the feet of those who bring the good news." (Romans 10:14-15)

Each of us makes assessments of the people around us, most of the time subconsciously. In the same way, when you work with Muslims, they will watch how you live. With this in mind, it is important that you are open about your faith. In the process of being open, it is good to emphasize your *personal* relationship with God because that concept is quite different from what is generally taught in Islam. Also, I stress that I worship the one true God, as opposed to three gods.

Another aspect that goes with this idea is the need for love and a servant heart. Once I heard of an Orthodox priest who said, "I am happy to be a friend but I do not want to be someone's mission project." Tell stories about how Jesus was a servant king and be a servant too. I would love to share the entire message of salvation every time I am with my Muslim friends and I am often ready to do so. However, sometimes a silent message of service speaks louder than my "well crafted" speech ever will.

Muslims see how Christians act. They see when we feed the poor, welcome the foreigner, and speak out for the rights of the weak and persecuted. A sincere and open heart, a willingness to listen with patience and charity, and sharing your home and heart with Muslims helps attract people to Jesus, the one who inspires such behavior in us, his disciples.

Physical Healing via Prayer in Jesus' Name

I have a theory about healing and mission: that in areas where the gospel has never been heard, we should go out with the power of the Holy Spirit, relying on God to work wonders. We are familiar with the scenario in the New Testament of an apostle preaching and then having his preaching backed up with miracles. In some of the places that

I have served, the gospel is just as new to the people as it was in the first century. If this is right, then we can expect God to do miraculous healings among Muslims, and by means of these healings, to validate that the good news is from God and not from men. Most Muslims in the United States have no idea what Christians actually believe. They are from locations where the gospel is hardly available, and they will not come to know the gospel without the efforts of American Christians.

I once heard of a man in the Middle East who regularly prayed for the healing of sick people. Before he prayed, he would ask that the entire family be present during the prayer. Then he would pray in Jesus' name and ask to leave right away. The reason he did this was twofold: First, so that all the family members witnessed that he was not using some type of magic spell, and second, so that when the healing took place, the family could discuss the miracle among themselves. On many occasions, after the sick person recovered, a family member would ask the person who prayed to return for a second time and pray for another sick person. Once again, the supplicant would ask everyone to attend but this time he would follow his prayer with a story about the power of Jesus. After the story, he would leave the home, expecting that the family would talk openly among themselves. Finally, if anyone in the family wanted to follow Jesus, hopefully, the rest of the family would be receptive to and supportive of the decision because of the healings,

It is important to remember here that the powerful role of physical healing in a decision for Christ is reported often by Believers with a Muslim Background (BMBs). That is, *they* were asked why they came to Christ, and a large number of them mentioned a supernatural healing.

Deliverance from Demons via Prayer in Jesus' Name

Similar to the point above, Jesus is the only one who can deliver someone from demonic attacks. I agree with those who say that prior to a baptismal service, a prayer of deliverance should be prayed over each person.[5] Indeed, this practice of carrying out an exorcism prior to baptism is something that the early church followed.

Many people in the Muslim world are acutely aware of the reality of evil spiritual forces in the universe. In the West we tend to think that everything can be explained using medicine or psychology (though the Bible clearly does not teach this), so we may need to place ourselves in another

---

[5] Rick Love, Muslims, Magic and the Kingdom of God: Church Planting among Folk Muslims (Pasadena, CA: William Carey Library, 2003).

frame of mind—one wherein angels and demons are understood to be an important, if invisible, part of daily life. This is especially true among folk Muslims, which is to say Muslims who have retained aspects of their pre-Islamic, indigenous religious practices.

Christians working among Muslims have learned this reality, and Muslims have encountered the power of Jesus' name after seeing dark spiritual forces submit themselves to that name. It is a powerful name, one that leads to spiritual freedom and liberation. This attracts many Muslims to Christ.

Dissatisfaction with Islam

An overarching guideline in ministry to Muslims is to avoid insulting the Qur'an, Islam, or Muhammad. While asking gentle, critical questions about the Qur'an and Muhammad is generally OK, it is usually better to focus on the positive message of God's love revealed in Jesus Christ. However, if a Muslim is already critical of their own faith, don't be surprised. But this is not permission for you to unload about what you think is wrong with Islam! In response, it is best to remain neutral or speak about the positive aspects of having a relationship with God. Also, ask questions. If criticism leads to a greater understanding of Islam and the world, it is something God can use to make Muslims aware that they might be better off choosing another path.

For instance, I met a Muslim tailor in India. Sitting on my sofa, he told me how many bad things had happened to him within Islam and that he was very unhappy. After listening for some time, my indigenous ministry partner and I explained that Jesus would not approve of what happened to him under Islam.

Islam teaches that the time of Muhammad's public career was an extraordinary time. The prophet governed all the people in justice and equity, and the Muslims were successful in all ways. Islam teaches that if a nation has Shari'a law, an Islamic government, and an Islamic population then every part of society should be healthy and prosperous. However, this is not the case in any location on earth. What Muslim country in the world today is an example of success in business, education, arts, and human rights? Moreover, an exploration of Muhammad's life will reveal a number of troubling things, such as his marriage to a child bride and his supervision of the extermination of the Jewish tribes of Medina.

The way of Jesus is different because the followers of Jesus are kingdom-oriented.

Governments rise and fall but God's kingdom is eternal. If governments write laws that allow grievous sins to take place or if they subvert truth and justice via negligence, that does not change our faith in God. Islam, on the other hand, rises and falls with its success here on earth.

So, when you hear a Muslim speaking critically about Islam or the Muslim community, tell them about a better way. Clarify that Christianity teaches an ethical system, but does not have a political system built into the religion, as does Islam.

Dreams and Visions

Dreams and visions seem to occur more often in places where the gospel is not readily available. Just do an Internet search for Muslims who had dreams about Jesus and you will find many stories. You can ask your Muslim friends if they have ever had a dream about God, Jesus or an angel; you might be surprised how often people say they have.

In the West people tend to assume that dreams are just the physiological byproducts of the sleeping brain. But many Muslims live according to a worldview that is closer to what we find in the Bible, a worldview that recognizes that dreams can be the mediators of divine knowledge.

In these dreams, Muslims often see Jesus or an angel, and they are often left with a mission such as visiting a certain person or obtaining a Bible. One woman was taught the Lord's Prayer in a dream. Another saw an image of a pastor with communion bread in his hand. In response, he left his country for a neighboring country with churches, walked into a church, and found the pastor holding the communion bread!

But remember that the dreams are never the end of the story. Dreams can cause the person to ask questions or find a Christian, but sooner or later the Muslim *must* have a real flesh-and-blood disciple of Jesus to instruct, pray, and (eventually) baptize the new believer. This was Paul's experience after his encounter with Jesus: He needed to meet Ananias to receive instruction, prayer, and baptism.

Special Truth in the Holy Bible

The Bible gives us some profound insights into the world we live in. We learn about ethics; we learn about how God is both just and merciful; and we learn about God's plan for the world he created. We also learn some deep truths about the human condition through our questions: How can humans be capable of great acts of heroism but also great acts of evil? How does humanity produce a Mother Theresa and a Hitler? The Bible tells us we are made in the image and likeness of God and so we are capable of great good, but we are also slaves to sin and death, alienated from God and each other, and therefore capable of great evil. The Bible's insight and wisdom regarding these difficult questions is most powerful.

Love of God in the Holy Bible

The God and Father of Jesus Christ is a loving and compassionate God. The Bible even makes the radical claim that *God* is love. Muslims can't say that. In Islam, God may love some people sometimes, but he may also scheme or deceive people. You're never sure what sort of response you will get from the inscrutable deity of Islam. How different is the God of the Bible who, while we were still sinners, sent Christ Jesus to die for us! Indeed, the unconditional, sacrificial love of God portrayed in the Christian faith is alien to the Muslim understanding of God. Furthermore, this Christian vision of God, who in his love and mercy came to be with us and die for us, has informed the preaching, thought, and prayer of BMBs around the world more than any other feature of the Christian faith.

My recommendation is to put a priority on equipping people with a Bible. There are stories of people who came to faith while they were trying to prove the Bible wrong. The Bible is powerful, and you will find this to be true when someone takes your advice and starts to read it. The Bible is available in almost every language and many different formats, so provide the version that your friend will most likely use and understand. And when you give your Muslim friend a Bible, treat the book with upmost respect. Wrapping it in silk or gift paper is good, and you can even kiss it before giving it away. Trust me, your Muslim friend will appreciate the gesture and be more likely to respect the Bible also.

THE SCRIPTURAL VANTAGE

So, know that Muslims are coming to Christ. But what does Scripture say about you and your Muslim neighbor?

There are four different attitudes people might have when considering work with Muslims in their communities. The first attitude is illustrated in the person of Moses. Moses became a great man of God, but he did not start out that way. In Exodus 3-4, Moses argued with God about God's plan for him to go to Pharaoh and lead the Israelites out of Egypt. In those verses, he asked God five times for another assignment.[6] He went out of his way to convince God that he had made the wrong choice in his selection of Moses to be the liberator of the Hebrews! Initially, Moses feared Pharaoh and the Egyptians, and my question to you is: Do you fear Muslims? If you are like many Americans, fear feels like a natural response to Islam. Sure, not all Muslims are terrorists or extremists—we are always reminded of this by the mainstream media and academics—but the reality is that almost all terrorists today are Muslims. I want to clarify that, for the Christian at least, fear cannot be a driving force, "...for God did not give us a spirit of cowardice, but rather a spirit of power and of love and of self-discipline" (2 Timothy 1:7).

The second attitude people might have about Muslims is indifference. The prophet Jonah fled Nineveh before God gave him a second chance to declare the Word of the Lord. Jonah was happy to tell his fellow Israelites what God had declared but was not interested in delivering the message to those of other nations. Are you indifferent to Muslims around you? Does their eternal destiny concern you enough to take action? Many Americans opt for this attitude, and call it tolerance or toleration. It can be summed up by saying, "You leave me alone, and I'll leave you

---

[6] Exodus 3:11,13 and 4:1,10,13

alone." But Christians are not called to "tolerate" others or leave them alone; Christians are called to love others, and that is true for the neighbor as well as the enemy.

The third attitude is intolerance. In Acts 10:9-48, we read that Peter was not willing to go to a Gentile house until God spoke to him in a vision. Good Jews were taught not to enter a Gentile house because they believed that they would become unclean. Thankfully, Peter understood what God meant when he said, "What God has made clean, you must not call profane."[7] This leads me to the question: Are you intolerant of Muslims? Do you look at them as God does or as many Westerners do?

The fourth attitude is based on ignorance. Ananias was a man used by God to do something great. In Acts 9 God told Ananias to visit Saul of Tarsus. Saul had a reputation of arresting and killing Christians. When Ananias was told to go, he asked God about it. He did not know that Saul had recently met Jesus in a miraculous way nor did he know that Saul would become the greatest missionary in the entire world. Are you ignorant of the fact that God will use BMBs to do great things for his kingdom?

---

[7] Acts 10:15

These four attitudes are at the heart of my reason for writing this book. I do not believe that any of these attitudes reflect mature Christianity. Christians are called to love their neighbors, and as Jesus taught in the parable of the Good Samaritan, your neighbor is not necessarily the person who is like you, of your own religion, or of your own ethnic group.[8]

SUMMARY

To sum up this chapter, Christians need to recognize that: (1) We as a Church have been negligent over the centuries when it comes to sharing the gospel with Muslims. (2) Islam is here to stay and will continue to grow throughout the West. (3) Some Muslims are indeed attracted to Jesus Christ and his community, and (4) The biblical and Christian response to this should not be fear, indifference, intolerance, or ignorance, but to love your neighbor as yourself.

With that in mind, let us now turn to Chapter 3 for some practices that the individual Christian can adopt in order to express love for their Muslim neighbor.

---

[8] Luke 10:25-37

Chapter 3

THE WITNESS: ONE BELIEVER

Chapter 1 focused on the need to demonstrate the gospel both in word and in deed. Chapter 2 concentrated on some of the historic mission activities of the church within Islamic countries; it concluded with biblical examples of the four ways many people view Muslims today. Chapter 3 explores various ways an individual can minister to Muslim people. The subsequent chapter focuses on ways a church can do the same.

"The task is so large! What am I able to do?" This question is born out of desperation and even defeat. But it is also a question that enters the mind more often than we care to admit. Satan would love for us to give up this type of ministry even before we get started. Too many people perceive Islam as impossible to penetrate. As stated in Chapter 2, there are about 1.5 billion Muslims in the world today, 2-3 million of whom live in the United States.

Dr. Clyde Meador, former executive advisor to the president of the International Mission Board—the mission agency of the Southern Baptist

Convention—wrote an encouraging article many years ago titled, "The Left Side of the Graph."[1] In his article, Meador encourages mission-minded Christians to persevere because even if positive results are not seen immediately, future like-minded workers will experience great growth as a result of the efforts made by the saints who came before them. In God's perfect time, he will move among a specific people group or location. As the Bible states, "I [Paul] planted, Apollos watered, and God brought the increase."[2]

There is a challenging Christian song titled, "I Can Only Imagine," by Mercy Me. It ponders what happens when a person arrives in heaven. In my own imagination, I think what might take place if each person, upon arriving in heaven, were to receive the full story of his or her faith journey. Perhaps we would learn about great-grandparents praying for us even though we had never met on

---

[1] The article appears as Chapter 9 of *Discovering the Mission of God, Supplement*, Mike Barnett, editor. (https://books.google.com.my/books?id=FFjjn9a0ubI C&pg=PT96&lpg=PT96&dq=left+side+of+the+graph+cly de+meador&source=bl&ots=bYugR6_bB_&sig=0TvvzC DDEdBuPK3H0yqNsD7B0qk&hl=en&sa=X&redir_esc= y#v=onepage&q=left%20side%20of%20the%20graph% 20clyde%20meador&f=false). Accessed on August 20, 2015.
[2] I Corinthians 3:6

earth. As we worship God face to face, we embrace each other, grateful for his mercy and grateful for the help of others along our faith journey. Now take that thought one step further. What would it be like if Muslims you never met on earth approached you in heaven and said, "Thank you. Your prayers and your ministry played a part in my being here to worship our Lord"? As they continue talking, they explain that the seeds of faith you planted grew to maturity years later. My friend, you *can* make a difference. You might see the change or you might not, but God does not allow his word to return void.[3]

The task in this chapter is to discuss several practical activities an individual can carry out while working among Muslim people. This will not be a complete list; however, the items mentioned below have produced positive results in the past. By the end of this chapter, you will have practical answers to the question, "What am I able to do?"

THE RIGHT PHILOSOPHY FOR WITNESSING TO MUSLIMS

My advice for working with Muslims is to remove walls of separation whenever possible. There are plenty of natural walls between Christians and Muslims, but they can be dealt with. An example

---

[3] Isaiah 55:11

of a natural wall is the cultural barrier between the two groups. Both groups believe the other group is wrong and offensive by doing certain things. Thus, the scripture to keep in mind at all times is 1 Corinthians 9:19-23.

> Though I am free and belong to no one, I have made myself a slave to everyone, to win as many as possible. To the Jews I became like a Jew, to win the Jews. To those under the law I became like one under the law (though I myself am not under the law), so as to win those under the law. To those not having the law I became like one not having the law (though I am not free from God's law but am under Christ's law), so as to win those not having the law. To the weak I became weak, to win the weak. I have become all things to all people so that by all possible means I might save some. I do all this for the sake of the gospel that I may share in its blessings.

There is a helpful article[4] that uses two words to describe the extremes of ministry among Muslims. The first term, *accommodationists*, applies to people who are willing to accommodate

---

[4] Duane Alexander Miller, "The Two Stream Hypothesis in Islamic Christianity: Accommodationist and Rejectionist" (scholarly research, *St. Francis Magazine*, 2009).

as much as possible within Islam. The second term, *rejectionists*, describes people who simply reject everything within Islam and Islamic societies and instead opt for traditional (often Western) Christianity. Between these two points of view are various types of ministry. I have no desire to tell a person the method to use; however, I can make two definite statements. Neither of the two *extremes* is advisable because there is room for many different approaches.

Three questions come to mind while reading the verses in 1 Corinthians. The questions are: (1) What am I *willing* to do so that I am able to share the gospel with others? (2) What am I *allowed* to do in the process of sharing the gospel? (3) What am I *asking a Muslim* to do when I invite them to become a follower of Jesus? Over the next few paragraphs, we will discuss these questions in greater detail.

The first question to consider is, "What am I willing to do so that I am able to share the gospel with others?" Paul took on some of the practices and customs of the people he wanted to reach, provided he did not break the law of God. I believe this is a practice that can be imitated by anyone who wants to work with Muslims. I cannot and will not tell you exactly how to do this, but instead encourage you to ask God what you are able to do. I have spent many years overseas adapting to the local culture and allowing God to stretch me in numerous ways.

Imagine a timeline drawn across a sheet of paper. The left end of the line represents when you were born, and the right end of the line represents the termination of your life on earth. Each one of us is on a spiritual journey in which God gives us opportunities to seek his face and follow him. Some people choose to follow him early in life, others later, and still others, not at all. Next, imagine a section of the line as the period of time when one is considering the truth of God's word and deciding how to respond to that truth. Once a person decides to follow Jesus, the journey does not end. In fact, God wants his followers to continue to grow into his likeness until the day they meet him face to face. In Christian terminology, this period of growth is referred to as growing in spiritual maturity.

Your Muslim friend is also on a spiritual journey, but what we call religious conversion does not usually take place at one given point in time (or on the line). Rather, for most BMBs the process of conversion is lengthy, sometimes taking years to result in a clear and informed confession in faith. Now should you expect them to live up to your level of spiritual maturity? Eventually, you want them to reach that level and beyond, but initially you must grant the friend grace by interacting with them at their level of spiritual maturity. For example, if your Muslim friend understands biblical stories incorrectly, do not give up or even argue. Instead, seek out a mutual belief and use that as a starting point. My desire is to walk alongside a person, helping them through the process of reaching a decision that results in growth toward spiritual maturity.

Here are two more practical examples of what this concept of grace means. First, Islam teaches that there were seventy people on Noah's ark while the Bible lists only eight people. However, for the sake of grace, when telling that story I suggest you bypass the conflict of the two different versions and focus instead on how the ark is a picture of salvation. Everyone on the ark was saved from destruction while everyone not on the ark was destroyed by God's judgment. The second example is taken from the story in Genesis 22 when Abraham took his son to be sacrificed. Muslims are very familiar with this story and will argue that it was Ishmael, not Isaac, who was on the altar that day. Although this is an important point, it is better to focus on the concepts of blood sacrifice and substitution. Just like the son (Isaac or Ishmael), each one of us should die for our sins, but God provided a substitute so we would not have to die. What good does it do to argue over Isaac and Ishmael while ignoring the message of salvation?

The second question from reading the passage in 1 Corinthians is, "What am I allowed to do in the process of sharing the gospel?" This question leads to several other questions. What must a person do or believe to be saved? What must we do or believe to remain faithful to the message we want to share? These questions open the topic of contextualization, for which I developed a few guidelines. First, there are many different opinions of how to carry out ministry. Second, God works through believers *and* unbelievers, and also through innovative *and* traditional methods. Third, each of us needs to evaluate continuously the effectiveness of our methods. Fourth, we must be willing to allow God to work through fellow workers even though those workers might not do things in the same way that we do them.

An example will bring this point out more clearly. There was a Muslim man who lived right in front of the mosque in a small Indian village. I met him shortly after he became a follower of Jesus. Because he lived in front of the mosque and all his neighbors were Muslims, he felt compelled to attend the mosque. As I sat and talked with him, he asked me, "Is it OK if I repeat the Lord's Prayer in the mosque?" He had just recently memorized that portion of scripture. My answer was an immediate yes. Then I proceeded to explain that he might need to change his practice of attending the mosque in the future, but for now, it is OK.

If I had told that man that he must attend a Christian church, his community (which is the lifeblood of Indian society) would have rejected him immediately. Added to that, he would have had to travel over two hours in one direction and spend fifty percent of his income on transportation to get there. In other words, I would have been building a wall. I mentioned at the start of this section that building a wall works against someone coming to and remaining in faith.

People build walls of separation between one another in many ways. When we judge others without first talking to them and trying to understand them, we build walls. A better approach is to try to understand the point of view of the people you want to reach. For example, Muslims dress in a certain way and have specific dietary requirements, neither of which, in and of themselves, violate biblical principles. Therefore, according to 1 Corinthians 9:19-23, we are permitted to do the same if it will help us to form a relationship. The point is not to become a Muslim, but to make Muslims more comfortable and receptive when we are talking with them.

The third and final question from the passage in 1 Corinthians is: What am I asking a Muslim to do when I invite them to become a follower of Jesus?

Yes, we want to see Muslims come to faith in Christ. It is also important that they become respected members of their families and a positive influence within the community. Of course, salvation is the most important issue, but it needs to be considered from a long-term perspective. Taking a person out of their community raises suspicions and fosters an image of we-versus-they. It gives people the impression that Christians have no problem destroying family bonds. If Muslims reject the new disciple of Jesus in their family, that is not surprising, and Jesus understood that this sort of reaction might take place. However, as Christians, it is our responsibility to do everything we can to help the new disciple of Jesus remain in good relationship with their family, as long as that does not compromise the integrity of the gospel.

Keeping this third question in mind, let us consider the issue of church. Within Islam, there may be an apprehension or even a stigma about attending a church. On the other hand, it is common for some Christians to invite their friends to church. In many cases, Muslims will not accept an invitation to church, but if someone does, please make sure the church is ready to receive your guest and that your Muslim friend is ready to experience your church. I suggest that either before or during a service, someone explain what is happening and offers to answer any questions. If you can introduce your Muslim friend to the pastor or preacher, that is also a good idea. Attending a church service will often be very surprising to Muslims as they see men and women worshiping God together—something they are not used to.

On the other hand, Muslims are much more likely to visit your house than your church. Officially, they are not supposed to drink from a cup that has been used for alcohol or from a pan that has been used for pork. Many, not all, assume that every Christian drinks alcohol and eats pork. Both of these issues are easily minimized by truthfully saying that both the cups and the pans are *hallal* (clean). By taking this extra step, it opens up a conversation about what Jesus did and how you try to live by his example.

In this section, based on 1 Corinthians 9:19-23, we explored three questions: What am I *willing* to do so that I am able to share the Gospel with others? What am I *allowed* to do in the process of sharing the Gospel? What am I *asking a Muslim* to do when I invite them to become a follower of Jesus? The fundamental guideline for each of these questions is to avoid building walls, but instead come alongside and join your Muslim friend on a faith journey. Next, we will discuss the importance of prayer and vision while working with Muslims.

KEY ELEMENTS FOR MUSLIM MINISTRY

My overarching philosophy is to avoid building unnecessary walls between Muslims and Christians. The previous few pages illustrate that point by addressing three main questions about the nature of ministry to Muslims. This section focuses on several key elements that every ministry must incorporate.

A God-given Vision

The first element necessary in Muslim ministry is a God-given vision. A vision is a road map to where the ministry is headed and what it will become. The vision helps define what the ministry will and will not do. My overarching goal is for everyone to hear and see a gospel presentation that is relevant to their lives. To achieve that goal, we must discern a vision that specifically defines what role the ministry will play.

There are two teachings worthy of mention concerning vision. The first is called *Z Thinking* and is part of the Omega Course,[5] developed by a group of people doing ministry in Russia. The second is a training course called *Acts 29*, a product of Dr.

---

[5] http://www.alliancescp.org/resources/omegacourse.html. Accessed on 31 July 2015.

Bruce Carlton's Project Thessalonica.[6] Z Thinking asks the question: What is the end vision and what steps are needed to get to that point? For example, let us say the goal is to have one hundred reproducing fellowships of BMBs in an area, all of whom are equipped to reach other Muslims in that same area. This statement becomes the "Z" (main goal). From that statement, one would work backwards until a starting point is reached. Of course, not everything will work exactly as planned, so flexibility and adaptation are crucial.

The Acts 29 teaching was developed as a direct result of ministry carried out in Cambodia. This teaching also emphasizes the end vision, but does so for multiple categories. For example, the ministry leader is encouraged to write an end vision statement for the categories of prayer, research, partnerships, platforms, evangelism, discipleship, and church planting. Once the vision is clear in each of these categories, quality action plans are written.

Prayer

Along with vision, prayer is another major element in Muslim ministry. Prayer is focused both on the workers and on the work that they attempt to do.

---

[6] R. Bruce Carlton, *29* (Singapore: Radical Obedience Press, 2003), 35-40.

One person, who is currently doing Muslim ministry, wisely recommends developing a prayer team of people dedicated to regularly taking all aspects of the ministry to God in prayer. If a prayer team is not available initially, start with just one person and pray for God to send more people. Furthermore, most churches already have prayer ministries of some sort, so try to share all your prayer needs with them.

Gospel Sowing

The third element in this list is highlighted in 2 Corinthians 9:6, which states, "But this I say: He who sows sparingly will also reap sparingly, and he who sows bountifully will also reap bountifully." Although the biblical context is about giving an offering, the principle is applicable in many different areas. One of those areas is making new friends and sharing the gospel with people from an Islamic background.

Networking

The fourth major element in Muslim ministry is networking. There are many benefits to interacting with like-minded people. Like-minded people are ones who understand the positives and negatives in your specific ministry. They are people who encourage you to press on and can give quality advice when needed. They are the type of people who pray powerfully on your behalf and are overjoyed when you do the same for them. Networking also is helpful for learning quickly where God is working in a certain area.

* * * * *

There is one more essential in this list, but before we mention it, let us consider how Satan attempts to keep people from fully implementing the previous four items. Because all these items are interrelated, balance is important. Satan tries to disrupt this balance by causing someone to focus wholly on vision or prayer while neglecting outreach, or vice versa. Still others spend too much time learning techniques or doing administrative work. Another way Satan works against effective ministry is by keeping ministries separate from each other, emphasized by the lack of trust among like-minded workers. An effective ministry will properly balance each of these four elements—vision, prayer, sowing, and networking —while constantly guarding against the work of Satan.

Finding a Person of Peace

The final element in Muslim ministry is finding a person of peace. The term is found in Luke 10:6

and mentioned in connection with the story of Jesus sending out seventy disciples in groups of two. The groups were given specific instructions by Jesus, instructions that are applicable to ministry today. Luke 10:1-9 states:

> After this the Lord appointed seventy others and sent them on ahead of him in pairs to every town and place where he himself intended to go. He said to them, "The harvest is plentiful, but the laborers are few; therefore ask the Lord of the harvest to send out laborers into the harvest. Go on your way. See, I am sending you out like lambs into the midst of wolves. Carry no purse, no bag, no sandals; and greet no one on the road. Whatever house you enter, first say, "Peace to this house!" And if anyone is there who shares in peace, your peace will rest on that person; but if not, it will return to you. Remain in the same house, eating and drinking whatever they provide, for the laborer deserves to be paid. Do not move about from house to house. Whenever you enter a town and its people welcome you, eat what is set before you; cure the sick who are there, and say to them, 'The kingdom of God has come near to you.'"

In this passage, Jesus was not teaching that door-to-door evangelism is the only way to share the gospel. Instead, he was emphasizing, among other things, the importance of finding men and women of peace. By "person of peace," I mean someone who will accept you and your message, and then introduce you to their network of friends and family members. Experience has proven that there are two types of people fitting this title. The first is a catalyst, someone who welcomes the evangelist and gathers others to listen to the gospel message. This person helps the evangelist make contacts with local people, who are otherwise difficult to meet. For example, a person of peace might invite you into their workplace so you can meet with people who are otherwise inaccessible. The second type of person of peace is someone who accepts the gospel and becomes a great witness within their own community. Typically, this person will be very bold and have a great vision for their community. Both types of people are extremely helpful in ministry. They will make ministry more exciting (albeit usually not easier) and provide new opportunities to share the gospel.

SUGGESTIONS FOR MEETING AND WORKING WITH MUSLIMS

Now that the essential elements are clear, let us consider several practical suggestions for ministry to Muslims. First, reach out only to Muslims about whom you truly care, and a great way to show you care about someone is by serving them. Serving happens in many different forms, sometimes planned and sometimes unplanned. Jesus is our ultimate example of what it means to serve someone else. Both his teaching and his actions showed the importance of this service.

Here is some wisdom I learned from a veteran missionary couple: Work with entire families when you can. When the leader of the home—and there is always a definite leader—is conscious of why you are approaching their family, reaching the family will become much easier. In addition, if the family does come to faith, there is already a structure for a house church as well as accountability. In many cultures, a church consisting of an extended family is the best place to start. Indeed, our idea of gathering many strangers together to be a church does not always fit in with non-Western societies. It is understood that this book is written for people working in the United States, but those we are trying to reach with the gospel are Muslims from other countries who are likely to have their unique understanding of community. Remember what I said earlier about not building walls? This family-based approach helps to avoid that. Although it might take a long time, the benefit of seeing a whole community come to faith is worth the wait. This doesn't always happen, but it does sometimes, and the Scripture has numerous examples of God saving entire families—think Noah and Cornelius, for instance.

Another suggestion for meeting and working with Muslims is to go to places where they might go. For example, visit specialty restaurants and grocery stores, or university campuses. Typically, it is not difficult to find Muslims. What is more difficult is to initiate a relationship that will become a long-term friendship. As I said before, providing a service is one way to do this. Another way is to become a learner and allow a member of the Muslim community to teach you something you do not know. Perhaps your future Muslim friend has a practical skill to teach or is willing to share history lessons with local children and adults. If that does not work, how about inviting your would-be friend and his family to a park or sporting event?

Other people have used social media to make contacts, or consulted published listings to locate people. Local mosques and Islamic centers often have days when they are open to the public for tours. Try going to one of these to learn more about the local Muslim community. The only limit is your imagination and motivation. Keep trying and praying. And when something happens (and it will), thank God for this achievement.

WAYS TO GET A RELIGIOUS CONVERSATION STARTED

There are many ways to share the gospel with Muslims. The following examples are drawn from around the world. Each one includes a brief explanation and footnote for further reference. Whether or not you use these methods or choose others, it is best to master only a few methods and learn to use them in a natural, conversational way. And, of course, you must strive to live what you preach, and preach what you live. But here is the key thing to remember: There is no method that is superior to genuine friendship and love, so don't think you need to read all the books in the footnotes before forming friendships with Muslims!

Kingdom Analogy

When Jesus spoke to people, he often used analogies that his audience could relate to. For example, he told Peter and Andrew that they would become fishers of men while they were working as fishermen.[7] At other times he used metaphors about farming and family when he was talking with villagers. When he was in Jerusalem during Holy Week, he had debates about Scripture and the Torah with scribes and priests—people who

---

[7] Mark 1:17

understood that world. With this in mind, we now have a choice to make. Either we can use the same analogies Jesus used and take time to explain their significance for today's audience or we can use more modern analogies that are consistent with the teaching of Jesus. Brian McLaren, in his book, *The Secret Message of Jesus,* made several suggestions. According to McLarenm, concepts like the dream of God, the mission of God, the network of God, and the revolution of God are all relevant in our time.

For the discussion in this book, let us focus on what Jesus said about the kingdom of God. While the idea of God's kingship was present in the Old Testament[8], Jesus greatly expanded on the topic in his teaching. The kingdom of God means the rule and reign of God over everything, both seen and unseen. Jesus' audience was familiar with earthly kingdoms and empires. Every Jewish person longed for the experience of their forefathers under the reigns of Kings David and Solomon. After the Jewish Kingdom fell, multiple other kingdoms rose and fell from power. When Jesus was on earth, the Roman Empire (a super kingdom) was the authority in charge. None of these kingdoms was perfect. Nevertheless Jesus

---

[8] Psalm 9:7-8, Daniel 4:34-35, Isaiah 37:16, Zechariah 8:22, and many more.

chose to use them as an image of God's relationship with mankind.

More specifically, let us consider what Jesus said about entry into the kingdom of God. One of the clearest passages of Scripture is John 3. In that passage Jesus told Nicodemus, a religious leader, that he must have both a physical and a spiritual birth to enter the kingdom of God. In other passages Jesus also emphasized the need for doing the will of the Father,[9] and having childlike faith.[10] The book of James summarizes Jesus' teaching by stating our need for both works (things we do) and faith (things we believe). In Chapter 6, I explain in greater detail the mystery of salvation.

The other requirement for entering the kingdom of God is righteousness. Moses was given the Law by God but no one was able to keep it completely. Therefore, some religious leaders misconstrued the law to make them appear righteous, and Jesus exposed their hypocrisy. Jesus also told a large audience that unless their righteousness exceeds that of the religious elite, they will not enter the kingdom of God.[11] This seemed like an impossible requirement to those

---

[9] Matthew 7:21
[10] Matthew 13:52
[11] Matthew 5:20

The Witness: One Believer

who were listening, but it echoed many other "impossible" requirements he made during the Sermon on the Mount (Matthew 5–7).

This caused a dilemma. On the one hand, people wanted to be part of God's mercy, healing, humility, and peace. On the other hand, Jesus told them they could not enter God's kingdom on their own. This dilemma was solved by Jesus himself. The key to entering the kingdom of God is repentance and faith. In Matthew 10:32, Jesus said that everyone who acknowledges him before men, he would also acknowledge them before his Father in heaven. Paul echoed this teaching in Romans 10:9, where he said, "If you confess with your lips that Jesus is Lord and believe in your heart that God raised him from the dead, you will be saved."

Islamic ideology states that if there is an Islamic government with Shari'a law and sincere Muslims for a population, then life should be very good. However, this is not the case anywhere in the world. But just like Muslims should not put their faith in an earthly government, neither should Westerners. Our faith is in God and our citizenship is above all in his kingdom, not any earthly kingdom or country. There are many ways you can use the kingdom of God analogy with your Muslim friend. The simplest way is to repeat the words and illustrations of Jesus, explaining any parts that are not easily understood. Read your Muslim friend some of Jesus' parables of the kingdom and ask them to tell you what they mean. Muslims are not used to critically reflecting on religious texts to figure out their meanings. Get them to do this with Jesus' parables. Also, read about how Jesus exemplified the kingdom of God by interacting with the weak, the poor, the rejects, women, Gentiles, and so on.

Eight Signs

The Kingdom Analogy method is often followed up by the Eight Signs study. This study emphasizes the dynamic of honor and shame when dealing with sin. Chapter 5 explains three ways to look at sin (innocence/guilt, power/fear, honor/shame) in much greater detail. The Bible refers to two roads and gates: The wide gate and broad road lead to destruction, and the small gate and narrow road lead to life. Drawing on the same metaphor, the Qur'an mentions the need to follow the straight path.[12] There are verses in the Qur'an that emphasize the importance of following the signs God has given us in order to remain on the straight path.[13] By definition, a sign is a physical and external representation of an internal and spiritual

---

[12] Matthew 7:13-14
[13] Surah Al-Fatiha 1:6

The Witness: One Believer 71

truth, and we want to focus on the spiritual meaning. God gave us the physical events so that we could understand the spiritual side of these signs. Each one of the eight signs becomes its own study. Each sign paints a picture that is completed in the person of Jesus the Messiah. Therefore, when it is time to talk about the eighth sign, Jesus, your friend will be able to understand how Jesus fulfilled each one of the first seven signs.

Following is an outline of the eight special signs:

A. The first three show us *what* God will do for us.

> Sign 1. The Holy Books: Torah/*Taurat*, Psalms/ *Zabur* and the *Injeel* (New Testament)
>
> Sign 2. Garment of Righteousness: Story of Adam and Eve being clothed by God.
>
> Sign 3. The Ark and Noah: There was only one door on the ark. God closed that door when He was ready to do so. Heaven is the same way.

B. The next two signs show us *how* God will do this work.

> Sign 4. Sacrifice: Through Abraham and his son, God provided a sacrifice.
>
> Sign 5. Blood: Through Moses and the tenth plague, the blood of the Passover sacrifice spared the people from judgment.

C. The last three signs show us *through whom* God will do this work.

> Sign 6. The Psalms and David: God established a covenant that the house of David would rule forever.
>
> Sign 7. The Sign of Jonah: When the people of Nineveh repented, God forgave them. Jesus used this story as a reference to his death, burial, and resurrection.
>
> Sign 8. Jesus the Messiah: Jesus fulfilled each one of the previous seven signs.

Camel Method[14]

This method is meant to gauge the spiritual interest of a hearer. Using this method, one is able to bridge into a gospel presentation. The method was developed out of the work of a BMB who uses many Qur'an verses as a bridge to the gospel. A person who worked overseas for many years later packaged the method into its current form. This method works best with someone who knows the Qur'an fairly well and puts their trust in that book. (Personally, though, when I use the Qur'an with Muslims, I am clear that I do not believe it is a divine book.) The method uses a single section of

---

[14] Kevin Greeson, *The Camel* (Arkadelphia, AR: WigTake Resources, 2007), 129-147.

the Qur'an to highlight the importance of Jesus. What is said in this section of the Qur'an is almost completely accurate according to the Bible.

The outline is as follows:

1. Jesus is holy.
   Al Imran (3) 42-47

2. Jesus has power over death.
   Al Imran (3) 48-54

3. Jesus knows the way to heaven.
   Al Imran (3) 55

If your friend shows interest about what you have shared in this section, the next step is to invite them to study the life of Jesus. It would be wise to use material that was written with Muslim ministry in mind.

SUMMARY

This chapter began with reference to an article titled, "The Left Side of the Graph," and then moved on to a key Scripture, 1 Corinthians 9:19-23. These verses lead us to three important questions: (1) What am I *willing* to do so that I am able to share the gospel with others? (2) What am I *allowed* to do in the process of sharing the gospel? and (3) What am I *asking a Muslim* to do when I ask them to become a follower of Jesus?"

These questions became the basis for the section on philosophy.

The philosophy of ministry was followed by five essentials to ministry among Muslims. The essentials are vision, prayer, gospel sowing, networking, and finding a person of peace. This was followed by several practical suggestions on how to meet Muslims and finally three evangelistic methods that have proven effective: Kingdom Analogy, Eight Signs, and the Camel Method.

In the next chapter, we broaden this topic of reaching individual Muslims by considering a group prospective. Chapter 4 is followed by an outline of the basic knowledge needed to work among Muslims, and the final chapter looks at the one true religion that God has laid out for each one of us.

Chapter 4
CHURCH MOBILIZATION

We as Americans tend to focus a lot on the life and thought of the individual, don't we? We also tend to think of many individuals coming together to form other secondary human configurations—communities. This is called individualism, and you can see it in every part of American culture, including our churches and religious life. Have you ever heard someone say they love Jesus but had no need for the church (that person's community)? Such a statement does not reflect biblical religion but modern individualism. Even the idea of "attending" a church by being alone in your room and watching the service on TV is an odd, individualistic slant on the Christian faith. (Of course, bedridden people who can't get up and go to church or have a minister visit them, have no choice but to worship in isolation.)

My point is that the church is something more than just a gathering of individual Christians. This is certainly the impression we get from a number of Bible passages. Consider Ephesians 1:22-23, "And God placed all things under his feet and appointed him to be head over everything for the church, which is his body, the fullness of him who fills everything in every way." This verse reveals that the church is nothing less than the fullness of Christ. Or, as one of the early Christian pastors[1] and martyrs put it, "You can't have God for your Father without having the church for your mother."

So, the church is special; it is unique; it, among all the societies and communities of the world, was founded directly by God. As such, the church in mission has abilities and gifts that are more than just the sum of the gifts of its members. The local church—whether meeting in an awe-inspiring cathedral or under a tree by the road—has a unique gift and vocation to carry out cooperatively in God's mission.

With this in mind, I want to explore how local churches can, as communities, reach out to their Muslim neighbors. Because a local church is more than just a gathering of individuals, that church's witness to Muslims is more than just the sum of what church members do on their own.

---

[1] Cyprian of Carthage

It is rare to find a church in America that, as a community, has a vision to share the gospel with Muslims. It is not rare to find individual Christians here and there who want to do this. This is to say that the material in the previous chapter about personal witness to Muslims is much more tested, tried, and developed than the material in this chapter. Figuring out how the churches of America (and the West in general) can best share the good news with their Muslim neighbors is still an open question. But, here are some ideas about where to start.

KNOW YOUR MUSLIM NEIGHBOR

Christians in America are sort of psychotic when it comes to ministry. On the one hand, much of our church leadership structure is modeled on that of corporate America. We approach planting churches in much the same way we approach opening a new franchise of a clothing store or restaurant. We research the population growth, languages, and socio-economic levels of the people of the city in order to discern where exactly the new church should be planted. But, on the other hand, we also love it when "coincidences" happen that, in retrospect, we understand to be the work of the Holy Spirit. Many of our favorite stories from the Bible seem pretty coincidental, such as when Jesus meets the Samaritan woman (John 4) or

Philip meets the Ethiopian (Acts 8). Those events did not come about because Jesus or Philip hired a research firm or did a demographic study.

So, which is it? Should we just trust in the Spirit to guide and make a way? Or should we follow the well-worn path of emulating corporate America in all things religious? I suspect that there is no one formula here that always applies. On the one hand, Christians need always to be aware that God can use them at any place and any time to carry out his work. On the other hand, if the church (or a significant group within the church) has a sense that God is calling them to minister among local Muslims, I would say that the Spirit has already been at work among them. At that point, it is good to begin by getting the lay of the land and doing some research, all the while being attentive to any guidance the Spirit provides.

With that in mind, here are some of the main questions you can begin with:

- Who are the local Muslims?
- Why are they here? Are they students, refugees, business people, converts, second or third generation Muslims, or something else?
- Where are they from? Some locations in the United States have large populations mostly from one or two countries (or regions in a

country); others have Muslim populations from all over the world.

- What sorts of Muslims are they—Sunni, Shi'a, Sufi, Wahabi, Salafi, Alawite, Ahmadi, secular? Be aware that different Muslims from different backgrounds interact with non-Muslims (and other Muslims) in different ways.

- How big is the local Muslim population? Is it growing quickly? (Chances are the answer is yes.) How well-established is it? Has your city or town had this presence for a long time, or is it new? Are there Muslim schools and mosques (often called Islamic Centers), and if so, how many?

- What are the needs of the local Muslims? This is a key question.

The list of questions is not exhaustive, but it is a good place to start. It is important to really get to know the history and culture (if not the language) of your Muslim neighbors. Most Americans tend to be ignorant and uneducated people when it comes to countries and peoples outside of the United States. Muslims know this and are used to it, so they will be pleasantly surprised when you know a few basic things about Pakistan or Turkey or Morocco or wherever they are from. This doesn't mean you need to read entire volumes of history about these places (though that is indeed a great thing to do), but do spend a couple of minutes every day keeping up-to-date on world events through websites or podcasts like *BBC World News* or publications like *The Economist* or *Foreign Policy*. Another good source of information on each country is *Operation World*. This book is organized in alphabetical order by country, and gives the reader some basic information on the state of Christianity in each.

One of the most frequent questions I get when I teach on Islam at churches is: What are Muslims like? And my answer is always the same: They are like Christians. Some are more devout, others less; some know their religion very well, others not so well; some are tolerant, others not so much. There is, however, an exception when it comes to violence. There is not an analogy for jihad in Christianity. I know people will point to the Crusades and say, "Look, Christians had jihad, too!" There is no comparison, though, because the Crusades were aimed at recovering land that for centuries had belonged to Christians and was taken away from them in an unprovoked war of aggression. Jihad, on the other hand, is an open-ended struggle aimed at ensuring the submission of every land and people to Allah and his Prophet. In any case, just as there is no such a thing as a generic Christian, there is no such thing as a generic Muslim.

Church Mobilization

This is precisely why it is so important to be informed about who your Muslim neighbors are and what they are like. The whole premise of this book is that loving your Muslim neighbor instead of ignoring or feeling bothered by them, must translate into action, specifically the action of sharing the best news of all with them—that they can be reconciled to God through Jesus the Messiah. If you know someone well, you will understand how to communicate this message to them in an intelligible manner.

I think about my kids here. I have three. They receive and show love in different ways: The oldest one loves to give and receive gifts; the middle one loves special gestures and time set apart, even if it is only to get ice cream; and the youngest one loves to play games and do puzzles. I know them, and I know how they understand the language of love. Know your Muslim neighbor. That is the first step.

ENGLISH AS A FOREIGN LANGUAGE

Language acquisition is a key need that many immigrants have, including Muslims. I know of several churches that host or coordinate English as a Foreign Language (EFL) classes of various levels. These classes offer excellent opportunities for educated lay Christians to spend quality time with immigrants (many of whom are Muslims), helping them to improve their language skills. My wife was a language helper for a young lady from China, who was a new Christian, and this was a great source of joy and edification for both women. If your church doesn't have enough people to set up an entire EFL program, then look around and find a church or EFL program in which you as a group can volunteer as teachers or language partners.

By "language partner" or "conversation partner," I mean someone who will meet with a language student on a regular basis (once a week is normal) in order to improve the student's language skills. That doesn't mean that the language partner needs to have a detailed curriculum, though. I don't want people to hear about the language partner option and assume that they need advanced training in EFL. I know of one language partner who just went through the Gospel of Mark, verse by verse, making sure the student understood the story and vocabulary. But, one could also use a magazine or a book, depending on the language skill of the student. Sometimes all that is needed is conversation. Choose a topic to discuss, and go for it.

Another language service that can be helpful is to focus on accent reduction. We've all had the experience of talking to someone who knows English well, but has a heavy accent and is thus difficult to understand. Helping Muslims reduce their accents can help them get better jobs and form better relationships with locals. Offering such classes or courses can be another way of loving your Muslim neighbor.

Ultimately, language studies offer many opportunities for people from your church to form authentic, loving friendships with your Muslim neighbors, and also to provide a useful service to them. Remember that the friendship in itself is the goal. It should be impossible for a disciple of Jesus to be someone's friend and not share the way of Jesus with them sooner or later.

INTERNATIONAL STUDENT MEALS

One key thing that draws young internationals to the United States is our system of higher education. Notwithstanding the many challenges facing higher education in the United States, our colleges and universities are generally considered to be some of the best in the world. People around the world know this and send their children here (and to Western Europe as well) for their college education. Moreover, it is wrong to suppose that only the elite universities receive foreign students, for even the local community college, the state university, and the second-tier private university receive substantial numbers of international students. Some enroll for only one semester, but many come to earn a degree. Some will end up working here or marrying an American citizen and settling here for the long run.

So, perhaps there is a college or university with substantial numbers of students close to your church, and if this is the case, it offers a venue for forming Christ-centered friendships with local Muslims. Coming from a foreign country can be a lonely business. International students will tend to naturally group with students from their home country, but many of them would sincerely like to have American friends. So, what sort of needs do international students have that their universities are not already meeting? Here are a couple of ideas:

Provide a weekly meal: I was briefly involved in a church that did this and was really impressed by the ministry. Every week, people from the church would make and bring food to their church hall, which was a couple of blocks from a medium-sized private university. A number of volunteers who were interested in forming Christ-centered relationships with internationals (not all Muslims, of course) would be at the various tables, and over the meal, we would have conversations about specific topics that had been determined ahead of time by the coordinators. It was nice to have a list of questions to chat about: What food do you like? Are you good at cooking? What would you like to see during your time in the United States? Tell me about your family back home. And so on.

This sort of ministry obviously takes a good amount of work. Some people need to set up the area; others need to cook and clean up; and then you need to have at least one person at each table to lead the conversation during the mealtime. Importantly, you need some people who will publicize this event, preferably *at* the university campus. (Normally, this would mean that you need someone who is a student or employee of that university.)

A meal ministry can yield numerous benefits. A person who has already been in the church complex for a meal is more likely to feel comfortable attending a religious service; the relationships formed can remain lively and fruitful for many years; students get an opportunity to practice and improve their English with native speakers; students get a homemade meal with people who care for them; students get free food. If you are doing this on a regular basis, it is possible to add special meals for Christmas and Easter, when it is natural to share explain why Christians find these two holy days to be times of fellowship and rejoicing.

There is another way to bless foreign Muslim students at the time of the holidays: Get host families from your church to welcome a foreign student over for the holiday—whether it is a religious or secular one. Holidays can be particularly challenging for foreigners. They see everyone having fun and hanging out with their friends and families, but often feel alone because they have no family nearby.

When hosting a Muslim, remember not to serve pork or alcohol as a basic rule. Some scrupulous Muslims may not want to eat food prepared in a kitchen where pork has been cooked, but I have found this to be very rare. The general Qur'anic teaching is that food is *hallal* (permitted, lawful) when a Christian (or Jew) serves it to a Muslim: "The food of the People of the Book is lawful (*hallal*) to you" (Al Maidah 5:5). If your Muslim friends are unsure about the food being *hallal,* you can point them to this verse in the Qur'an. Believe it or not, discussing food prohibitions can be a great gateway to talking about Jesus, as he certainly had some things to say on the topic.

You can host a Muslim student during Ramadan. This is a lunar month of the Islamic calendar, and during this month, Muslims are supposed to fast from sunup to sundown. If you have a substantial number of Muslim students, break the fast with them. This is a good opportunity to experience what the Muslim fast is like, as it involves not drinking anything from sunup to sundown, which is arguably more difficult than not eating. On another level, if you have a spare room in your home, why not open it up for an international student to live with you?

REFUGEE SETTLEMENT

Many of the least stable countries in the world are majority-Muslim countries, and a large number of the refugees from those countries eventually settle in the West, including the United States. Any person who is persecuted for their political or religious beliefs may well end up in the United States.

Normally, refugee settlement is contracted out from the federal government to various organizations that settle refugees. This is where people from your church come into the equation: These organizations are often stretched very thin and can't meet all the needs of the refugees they are settling. So, they try to connect refugees with locals who can help them with a host of challenges. These include getting the phone connected, registering kids for public school, applying for jobs, getting a driver's license, and various other bureaucratic tasks. Remember also that the American medical system is incredibly complex, and refugee families may need help with it. Helping a family learn about cultural habits is also worthwhile—shaking hands, habits of cleanliness (in many parts of the world, body odor is considered normal, and people just ignore it, for instance), how to work an air conditioner or heater, avoidance of littering, and so on.

While many of the refugee settlement organizations are affiliated with a Christian denomination (Catholic, Episcopal, Lutheran), they are not allowed to evangelize the refugees they are settling. Furthermore, anyone who volunteers to help them must likewise agree to this. This rule does not come from the refugee settlement organizations, by the way; it comes from the government. (Yes, the Christian roots of this nation that formed an ethic of welcoming the hungry and the persecuted have led to the mind-boggling reality that the Christian message cannot be shared with people who come here because of those Christian roots.) However, your relationship with the settled family will hopefully last well beyond any volunteer period with the organization. Once that period is over and you have been a blessing to the refugee settlement organization and also to the family, you are free to speak about your faith in Jesus Christ as one friend to another.

Remember that while a lot of refugees are Muslims, not all of them are. So, if you are put in contact with a family from some other religious background, you should embrace that opportunity too. There are very few ministries where you know for sure that you will interact with Muslims and Muslims only.

MUSLIM-CHRISTIAN DISCUSSION GROUPS

Interreligious dialogue is quite popular today, especially in the more liberal Christian churches. Some people have the idea that the age of evangelism is over, and that it has been replaced by interreligious dialogue. Unfortunately, at the heart of how many people envision interreligious dialogue is the naïve and baseless conviction that if Muslims and Christians understand each other better, they will have peace and harmony. I say this is baseless and naïve because I believe (and the church confesses) that the root of violence, war, and animosity is not ignorance of others, but the spiritual death that the Bible calls sin. A lot of evangelical Christians are aware of this and therefore assume that interreligious dialogue is of no use to them.

But let me suggest that interreligious dialogue can exist side by side with evangelism, neither replacing it nor being replaced by it. Envision your pastor contacting the imam of a local mosque or Islamic center and suggesting something along the following lines: "Let's get together once a month, and we'll alternate between topics: One month, you choose the topic; the next month, I will. We'll each have twenty minutes to summarize our positions on the topic (no interruptions at all), and then the people who are attending (folks from your mosque and my church) will have time to ask questions of both of us."

Interreligious dialogue is valuable because it serves as a forum for education and enables both Christians and Muslims to see that they have inaccurate understandings of each other's faith. But the facet that is most attractive to me is that the folks from your church can really get to know and build relationships with local Muslims; perhaps they will continue those relationships outside the formal interreligious dialogue. Relationships are where life is shared, and since Christ is your life, then he will be shared; call that evangelism, if you like.

Now this book is written for Christians, but I need to interject a note here for any Muslims who may be among my readers: I am happy that you are reading the book! This is not some sort of secret plan that we Christians are trying to hide. Dear Muslim leader or imam, you have much to gain, and nothing to lose by taking part in this sort of interreligious dialogue. Such a relationship would help people to see how tolerant and peaceful Islam can be; it would help the people of your mosque better understand what Christianity in America is and provide them with a peaceful and calm context for asking questions.

But back to my Christian audience! There is one caveat about interreligious dialogue. Christians should be aware that many Muslims in the United States (especially leaders) are keenly aware of how suspicious people are of Islam. And so, when they answer questions, they whitewash some less savory facets of Islam. I would point out that Christians do this, too. Rather than thinking of this practice as lying, understand it as putting one's best foot forward. When Christians are asked about women in the Bible, for example, they don't cite Ecclesiastes 7:28 on how the author could find one righteous man among 1000, but not a single righteous woman among 1000 women. No, we focus on how Jesus had women followers and how he vindicated the woman caught in adultery. Muslims do the same thing, and be aware that this may happen. Just because you hear an imam (or pastor) say something, that doesn't mean it is the whole story. You have the right and obligation to ask questions and dig deeper.

THE INTERNET

When a Muslim has a question about Jesus, the Bible, or anything Christian, it is likely that they will look for answers on the Internet. Does your church's website make it clear that your pastor or another leader is eager to answer the questions of local Muslims? If Muslims want a Bible in their own language, does your church's website let them know that you can get it for them? Most churches have a running class on the basics of the Gospel. Why not advertise on your website that Muslims who want to know about Christianity would find this class helpful and are welcome. If a Muslim student doesn't have transportation, does your church advertise free transportation for Sunday morning worship and have someone in place who can provide the transportation? Thanks to Google, Yahoo! and other search engines, just including these words on your website—Muslim, Islam—will make your church visible to the local Muslim seeker.

SUMMARY

"And everything you do, do it as unto the Lord," said Paul.[2] While your end goal may be seeing Muslims hear, understand and accept the gospel, remember that all of your service to Muslims should be done with excellence: the lesson preparation for English classes; the food cooked for a meal; the application for food stamps—whatever it is that you are helping with. Also, remember that these ideas are meant to meet real needs that people have (in itself a Christian thing to do), but also to allow for the formation of deep friendships

---

[2] Colossians 3:23

through which you can share the person of Christ most authentically and deeply. And remember, the mark of genuine friendship is that it is unconditional. So even if your Muslim friend avoids speaking about faith or religion, do not abandon them. What if God had abandoned you because for years you were not open to hearing his voice or obeying him? Love your Muslim neighbor as yourself! On a final note, be sure to keep your church's prayer ministry in the loop from the time you begin researching the local Muslim population through the development of action plans and the provision of services.

Chapter 5
THE KNOWLEDGE

The previous two chapters focused on ways in which individuals and churches can reach out to Muslims. The practical ideas in those chapters could be implemented immediately. In this chapter, we focus on what a person needs to know about Islam and Christianity for maximum effectiveness.

The goal of every Christian should be to assist in the process of a person entering the kingdom of God. Jesus constantly spoke about the kingdom of God, especially in relation to the requirements for entry. When one closely studies Jesus' message, it is clear that Jesus used different approaches with different people. This chapter is not only about specific knowledge, but also about the key to making the gospel understandable for specific audiences. There are two extremes that should be avoided: One is to believe a Christian worker does not need to learn anything about Islam and the other is to believe a Christian worker needs to know everything about Islam. The first most likely will result in minimal (if any) fruit, and the second will result in years of study at the expense of sharing the gospel. This chapter will provide sufficient knowledge to get started, and, hopefully, help you develop an interest in further research.

SOME OF YOUR MUSLIM FRIEND'S BELIEFS

There are at least three important factors that have a significant impact on all aspects of doing ministry. These factors are foundational and therefore worthy of mention before progressing any further. First, many Muslims believe that everyone in the West is a Christian. In most major world religions (and several minor ones as well), children are born into the religion of their parents. Therefore, when a Muslim with limited exposure to Christianity considers this topic, they assume that everyone in the West must be from a single religion. Contrast this with the evangelical teaching that while children may be raised in the church, at some point they eventually need to make a personal decision to live as a Christian.

Taking the Muslim worldview a step further, one starts to understand why Muslims are critical of Christianity. When the negative aspects of Western culture are inaccurately categorized as "Christian" (movies, TV shows, celebrity scandals, Las Vegas, abuse of alcohol), it is no wonder people want nothing to do with the religion. Often, the positive aspects of Islam become a point of national pride while any negative parts are minimized or ignored. As a result, the worst of Western culture is compared to the best of Islamic culture, resulting in a rejection of Christianity. Therefore, while in the company of Muslims, some Christians use a different term to refer to themselves. For example, some people call themselves "a follower of Jesus" or "a follower of the way."[1] If you prefer to use the word Christian, make sure that your Muslim friend understands what this word means. In fact, this can be a great opening for sharing the gospel. You might say something like, "I'm a Christian. What do you think that means?" It is also a good idea to state that you go to church, read the Bible, and pray on a regular basis. The point is not to boast about your religious life, but to communicate to your Muslim friend that you take these issues seriously.

A second overarching truth is that Islam is a community. A mantra that is known throughout the Islamic world is, "Me against my brother, me and my brother against my cousin, and me and my cousin against the world." This means that a person will argue with their family member until a more threatening enemy arises. At that time, the two family members in dispute will suspend their

---

[1] Acts 9:2

argument and join forces to work against that enemy until the common enemy is defeated, after which the two will resume the original argument.

The understanding of community in this sense is very different from the typical American worldview of individualism. In a society based on community, decisions are made with others in mind. It is not uncommon for a 35-year-old Muslim married man to check with his father before making an important decision. This shows honor to the father and maintains unity within the group. From a Western perspective, intimidation is evident within Islam. I truly believe that some Muslims are curious about Christianity, but are afraid to ask about it. They do not fear what they might find in Christianity as much as they fear what might happen to them if a family member or religious leader were to learn about their curiosity. This attitude apparently stimulates high numbers of anonymous Internet inquiries on Christian websites.

Given the importance of family to Muslims, it is important that Christians work within a Muslim community system as much as possible. In Chapter 3, I talked about a champion of the faith who saw amazing results by working through the family structure. Do understand the spirit in which I make this suggestion. I am not saying to neglect university students or single individuals.

There are many examples of individuals coming to faith and being the catalyst for entire movements of God. Having said that, work hard to establish a presence among the whole Muslim community and families within that community.

The third overarching truth is that many times Muslims try to raise four or five big topics, all at the same time. This happens especially when a person either feels threatened or wants to argue. When that happens, tell the person that each item raised is important, but it is possible to deal with only one item at a time. Often this response is met with understanding. Those who are unwilling to stop badgering often do not want to hear an answer or allow others in the audience to hear it.

Consider that the Bible itself is a progressive revelation. For example, the first four words of the Bible, "In the beginning, God," start the story about God. And as we continue to read the entire Bible, we learn much more about God. Of course, the stories of Jesus and the New Testament are transformational, but those stories are enhanced when one understands Old Testament concepts. There is no doubt that the followers of Jesus understood that he was Lord and Savior. What makes this fact even more noteworthy is that Jesus' followers were monotheistic Jews.

In summary, the three overarching influences discussed in this section are: (1) Muslims believe that everyone in the West is a Christian; (2) Islam is a community; and (3) Muslims, in conversation, often attempt to argue many different points at the same time. Awareness of these potential difficulties will allow you to prepare for and hopefully facilitate a constructive conversation with your Muslim friends.

AN ANALOGY FROM INDIA

We are about to discuss seven key issues that often come up in conversation with Muslims. However, before moving forward, there is one more foundational piece to our discussion that I would like to share, which I will do through an analogy I heard from a friend in India:

> To know me is to know how much I like Indian chai. I drink it every day, and when I travel, I carry the exact ingredients with me. My favorite version is a recipe that was given to me many years ago. Each morning, I add the following to one liter of water: Taza brand tealeaves, milk powder, sugar, cardamom seeds, fresh ginger, and cinnamon bark. The combination sits on the stovetop until I think it is ready. However, before I can drink the chai, there is one more important step; I must strain it. Although the flavor would be good, I do not want to drink loose tealeaves or cinnamon bark, so I need to throw that part away.

> The lesson is that each person has a life filter. Islam is a way of life that has positive features. However, not everything in Islam is redeemable (this same statement is also true for cultural Christianity). Some parts of Islam need to be discarded. Therefore, in this analogy, the filter or worldview is very important. Each person has had various teachings and life experiences that flavor their lives but ultimately are contrary to the teaching of the Bible. In other words, the filter in this illustration represents the Bible. Therefore, it is important for each person to know and rightly understand what the Bible says. Using something other than the Bible or only pieces of the Bible to filter one's life experiences is like using a chai filter with gaping holes.

What is the lesson from the experience of this Christian in India? When an issue between Islam and Christianity is raised, pull out your strainer and work through the following checklist. First, identify a specific practice within Islam. Second, compare it to biblical principles. Third, condone the Islamic practice if it does not contradict the Bible. Fourth, explain the practice in light of biblical teaching, and fifth, drop the practice if it contradicts the Bible. An example some missionaries have faced is fasting during Ramadan: Should BMBs continue this fast in order to preserve harmony with their family? Is fasting during a particular season of the year unbiblical? The result has been that the BMBs continued to fast during Ramadan, but their intention was no longer to gain merit before God (as it had been before), but rather to intercede for the salvation of their compatriots.

INTRODUCING THE MAJOR TOPICS

The remainder of this chapter addresses seven key doctrinal subjects. Experience teaches that it is one thing to believe something and another to defend that belief in a real life situation. Space does not allow me to give a complete accounting of each of the issues. If you want to learn more about them (and I encourage you to do so), a good place to start is the Answering Islam website (answering-islam.org). Also, none of the comments listed below is meant to be the final or best voice on any one topic. Although truth does not change, the path to finding the truth may take many forms. For example, one person's quest for the true God might start with the beauty of nature while another's might be the study of religious books. Each conversation is just as unique as the person to whom you are talking. Therefore, there is no such thing as a stock answer to the questions raised by each topic.

The seven issues are the Holy Scriptures, God and Allah, Sin, the Person of Jesus, the Tri-Unity of God, the Crucifixion, and the One Gospel. Each topic will be examined in four steps. First, stating the issue; second, explaining how Muslims view that issue; third explaining the Christian understanding of the same issue; and fourth, listing one or more practical responses that can be used during a conversation.

Holy Scripture

One of the most common objections that Christians face when speaking with Muslims is the charge that the Bible has been changed. According to Islam, the original manuscripts were accurate, but, at some time (no one is able to say when) changes were made to those manuscripts. Actually, the circular argument that accompanies this idea is that Christians follow an inaccurate book while simultaneously changing the book to fit their religious beliefs. A Muslim man approached me in India stating that he could prove the Qur'an was correct and the Bible was not. He proceeded to tell me that Lot, the nephew of Abraham, was a good man in the Qur'an (considered one of the prophets) yet in the Bible, he is not a good man. I waited for the man to continue his argument, but, in fact, that was all he had to say. In response, I told him he proved the two books were different in this single point, but he did not prove anything else. Just like this man, no Muslim is able to answer the questions: When was the Bible changed? By whom? How? And which specific parts were changed?

The Islamic argument states that the Qur'an is God's final revelation to man, and, therefore, no other book is necessary. Sometimes, Muslims ascribe changes to the Bible to the original audience, and other times, they blame early Christians who confessed Jesus as Lord. By posing the argument in either of these two ways, the writers of the Bible, who are all prophets in Islam, remain unflawed (Islam generally teaches that all prophets are sinless), and the Hebrew people look bad for having disobeyed the written word of God.

In contrast, the orthodox Christian position is that the prophets and apostles wrote the scriptures under the guidance of the Holy Spirit. Although each person incorporated his own unique style, the Holy Spirit guided the author to write exactly what was supposed to be written. The Bible was written by about forty different people over a period of fifteen hundred years, yet a central theme runs throughout the Bible, that of Jesus the Messiah. Other striking proofs attesting to the accuracy of the Bible are fulfilled prophecy, the personal humility and honesty of the writers (they write about their own sins), and the central focus on God. As stated by Robert Saucy, "A great deal of research and study has been conducted from every possible angle on the Bible and yet it remains unscarred."[2]

Although it is possible to raise issues about the Qur'an via historical and textual evidence, that type of argument erects a wall that is almost impossible to remove. Therefore, it is better to point out the positive and overwhelming evidence supporting the Bible while not talking negatively about the Qur'an. The following are several more ways to respond to a Muslim who is willing to discuss this issue.

Muslims divide the Bible into three sections, the Taurat (first five books), the Zabur (Psalms), and the Injeel (New Testament). They do not formally recognize the other books of the Old Testament, but the Qur'an does draw also from extra-biblical Christian traditions and writings. Sixty-nine times the Qur'an states that some or all of these three main sections are trustworthy.[3] Five *ayat* (verses) in the Qur'an state that the previously revealed divine books (a term used for the Bible) were misrepresented.[4] These verses do not identify the "changed" text, but state that

---

[2] Robert Saucy, *Scripture* (Nashville, TN: Word Publishing, 2001), 75-85

[3] Al Baqarah 2:41, 2:181, Al Imran 3:3-4, Yunus 10:64, 94-95

[4] Al Baqarah 2:75, Al Imran 3:78, An Nisa 4:46 ff.

people, knowing the original text, taught something different. If your friend trusts fully in the Qur'an, allow them to carefully read these verses. Hopefully, this will increase their desire to explore the Bible.

The next approach requires the following background information:

(1) The Qur'an was first enunciated between 610 and 632 A.D.

(2) In Surah Al Araf 7:188, Muhammad is called a person who warns others of the truth.

(3) Added to this, the Qur'an has only good things to say about the Bible.

(4) The Bible that we read today is taken from the oldest manuscripts possible.

(5) To illustrate, the Codex Sinaiticus is a handwritten complete copy of the New Testament and partial copy of the Old Testament. It is over sixteen hundred years old.[5] In addition, Greek and Hebrew language scholars today refer to the Codex Sinaiticus and even older material when making a modern translation.

Now that we know the relevant facts, we can formulate a case for the veracity of the Bible. Our

---

[5] http://www.codexsinaiticus.org/en/ (2 Sept. 2015)

modern Bible is derived from texts dated 350 A.D. and earlier. The Qur'an was first recited by Muhammad some 250 years after that time (610-632 A.D.) and claims to warn people about the truth. So, if the Bible has been changed, when could it have happened? The Qur'an does not warn its readers about a corruption of the biblical text, so logically that means it could only have happened after 632 A.D. Any changes prior to this date should have been mentioned in the Qur'an itself. However, the modern translations of the Bible are produced from sources dated prior to the Qur'an. In other words, if a person claims to believe the Qur'an, then, logically, that same person should believe the Bible.

In summary, this section offers several responses to the claim that the Bible is corrupt. One is to mention the evidence supporting the Bible. (There is a great deal more evidence than could fit into this short section.) The other two responses are the fact that the Qur'an speaks only positively about the Bible and that the modern translations are derived from sources much older than the Qur'an itself. Finally, if all these arguments are not effective, ask your friend how it can be that God is powerful enough to create the entire universe, but not strong enough to protect his written word.

God and Allah

Within the realm of Christendom, an active debate has been going on regarding the term *Allah*. It is not my desire to participate in this debate, but I do have an opinion that I hope to make clear over the next few pages. There are several definite do's and don'ts in Muslim ministry. One of them is to avoid spending your time arguing about a perfect method while neglecting to engage the people who need a Messiah. Another is to refrain from attacking another person's ministry while attempting to fulfill the task God has laid out for that specific person. Muslims will not be attracted to Christ and his community if they perceive that our disagreements are stronger than our unity.

When Muslims use the term *Allah*, they have a particular understanding. Muslims worship Allah and they are quick to defend his name. However, they believe Allah is unknowable and unreachable. Muslims officially will not allow Allah to come to earth (in the form of a messiah) because he might become unholy. Many Muslims do not differentiate between the realms of the spiritual and the physical. This topic will be discussed in greater detail in the next section, but for now, just understand that the result of this thinking is what keeps Allah in heaven rather than coming to earth as the Son of God did. This confusion leads to an even greater dilemma because now Muslims must live up to an impossible standard. Islam does not have anyone who, like Jesus, was tempted in every way and yet did not sin.[6] Nor do they have someone who can both reach heaven and touch earth. This is what the prophet Job cried out for during his time of misery. Job understood his and our need for a mediator "who may lay his hand on us both."[7]

In Islam, names for each of Allah's ninety-nine different attributes are given. Some Muslims even use the ninety-nine names as a good luck charm. For example, some Muslims in India repeat the fourth name of Allah, *Al Quddus* ("the holy one"), one hundred times a day after Friday prayers, believing this will bring them peace of mind and safe travel.[8] A Christian would say that the God of the Bible is holy, but that his name is not to be used to invoke good luck!

Let us take a moment to consider an issue of terminology. The word *Allah* is actually much closer to the Hebrew word found in the Old Testament, *El*, or its commonly used plural form, *Elohim*. In fact, the two words derive from a similar root because Arabic and Hebrew are both Semitic

---

[6] Hebrews 4:15

[7] Job 9:33

[8] Parves Dewar, *The Names of Allah* (New York City: Viking Press, 2003), 11.

languages and often overlap. Compare this to the English usage of the word *God*, which has no resemblance whatsoever to any word in the Bible, whether Hebrew, Aramaic, or Greek. If we want to tell BMBs that they cannot use an Arabic word they are familiar with, then we should be honest and stop using the Germanic word we are familiar with (*God*) and start using a word from the Bible: *YHWH, Elohim*, or *Theos*.

In addition, there are lessons from the history of the church's mission. Generally, when Christian missionaries encountered an unreached people group, they inquired about the sky god or creator god, and then went on to explain that this was the one true God, and that he sent his Son into the world to be our Savior. Indeed, this is precisely why we, speaking English, which has so much Germanic influence, use a Germanic word for the deity. Finally, consider yet another point. The word *Allah* actually predates Islam. Arabic-speaking Christians and Jews had been using the word for centuries before Islam came around. The most respected Arabic translation of the Bible, which was the work of a highly skilled team of Presbyterian missionaries and scholars working in the nineteenth century, utilizes the word *Allah* for "God."

On the other hand, Jesus taught that there is a separation between the physical and the spiritual worlds.[9] He said that if a person ate with unwashed hands, it would not affect their spiritual condition. The items that do affect a person's spiritual condition, he said, are issues of the heart.

The aim, then, is not to avoid using the word *Allah* necessarily, but rather to introduce the Muslim to a deeper and more Christ-centered understanding of who Allah is. He is not, in fact, the one who called Muhammad to be his final prophet. Rather, he is the God and Father of our Lord Jesus Christ.

In conclusion, the church through its missionary endeavor has settled this question. There is no need to rehash old arguments or to stop using the word *God* in English. In the same way, we should not hold Muslims to a standard that we ourselves are not willing to live by.

Finally, a bit of common sense: If you do not feel comfortable saying "Allah," then try using one of his other titles, such as the Creator or the Lord. Muslims understand these terms and will not find them insulting or strange.

Sin

A Muslim will not argue much over the topic of sin but may not even mention it in conversation. There

---

[9] Matthew 15:11

are several reasons why this is true. First, *sin* is a negative term and something most people do not want to admit to. Second, the word *sin* carries the connotation of judging, which is taboo, especially when it is applied to someone directly. Although both Muslims and Christians use the word *sin*, the two groups understand the word differently. I will next summarize the issue of sin, then give the Islamic view followed by the Christian view, and finally conclude with some practical guidance.

The topic of sin is foundational because it has ramifications for how one views life and redemption. For example, if God forgives every sin automatically (a belief of some Muslims), there is no reason to live a good life. Or, if God accepts only good works, we are all in competition to do better than the next person, and pleasing God becomes a side issue. The options and corresponding ramifications are limited only by one's imagination.

In short, Islam teaches that Allah's grace will cover almost every sin and that Allah does not need a sacrifice in order to forgive people. From this first point onward, there is a series of intertwining beliefs leading to false understandings. I will try to list them in some semblance of order.

Muslims are flexible when it comes to defining the word *sin*. Although honest Muslims admit they are sinners, their sins do not make them worthy of eternal punishment in hell. Since sin is not a grave issue, and Allah can forgive any sins as he sees fit without the need of an atoning sacrifice, there is really no need for a savior. Next, if one does not need a savior, then Jesus need only be a good teacher, a role model, and a prophet. The Christian claim is that Jesus' death on the cross reconciles us to God and leads to the forgiveness of our sins. This strikes most Muslims as, at best, exotic, and, at worse, blasphemous. Another important item is that Islam believes the first sin of Adam was only a localized event, and his sin did not affect anyone else. In fact, Islamic theology states that God made man weak and forgetful.

In addition, when Muslims hear the word *grace*, they often think of what Christians call cheap grace. *Cheap grace* is a term first used by Dietrich Bonhoeffer in *The Cost of Discipleship*. In his words, cheap grace is forgiveness without repentance,[10] or put another way, it is when a person acts in any way they wish, assuming that God will forgive their actions. The people of Islam emphasize Islamic law and believe in God's grace, but add the stipulation that the grace of God must be earned in one way or another. As with every

---

[10] http://www.goodreads.com/quotes/423945-cheap-grace-means-grace-sold-on-the-market-like-cheapjacks (Accessed on 2 September 2015).

religion except Christianity, Muslims end up working for their salvation instead of receiving it from God. Or, if they are forgiven by God, then that forgiveness is arbitrary and one can never know with confidence whether they have been forgiven.

In contrast to the Islamic teaching, the following is a short review of the Christian doctrine. The Christian definition of *sin* is anything we say, do, or think that is against the will of God. Alternatively, one could say that sin is any misuse of the free will God gives to mankind. The sin of Adam has affected both humanity and the created world. As for the creation of mankind, because God is entirely pure, he could not have made an impure person or world. Both Adam and the world he was placed in were perfect. However, because of sin, both we and the world we are born into are no longer perfect. It is incorrect to say that a perfect God made anything imperfect. When humans first misused their free will and sinned, death entered into the cosmos: spiritually, relationally, and ontologically.

The Apostle Paul addresses the issue of grace very clearly in Romans 6. He states that true followers of Jesus turn from sin because they have received the grace of God, and if a person continues to sin with the idea that God will forgive them, then that person is probably not a true follower of Jesus.

At this point, let us take a moment to consider how the Bible addresses the reality of death and its offspring, sin. The three predominant facets of death in the Bible, each of which speaks to a different emphasis, are guilt/innocence, fear/power, and shame/honor. There are not three different gospel messages to address each one of these groupings, but by knowing this distinction, one can formulate a presentation of the gospel to address the receiver's worldview. Each society and family group emphasizes one or two of these viewpoints while minimizing the others. Although we are able to make certain generalizations, it is best to get to know the person you are speaking with so that your presentation is as meaningful as possible.

Guilt and Innocence. In Western countries, people's worldviews are based predominately on the concept of guilt and innocence. In this view, the written law or rulebook determines what is right and wrong, and everyone is expected to live by that standard. When a rule gets broken, society becomes upset and expects an authority figure to do something about it.

In Genesis 3, God gave Adam and the woman a rule, telling them which fruit to abstain from in the garden. Although the woman ate the forbidden fruit first, Adam was close enough for the woman to hand him the fruit for him to eat, and thus both of our first ancestors were guilty of breaking God's rule and deserved to be punished.[11] Gospel presentations you could use to emphasize this view of sin are *The Roman Road, Four Spiritual Laws*, and many others. One of the most relevant Bible verses about sin is John 1:29, "Behold, the Lamb of God who takes away the sin of the world!"

Fear and Power. In places such as South America, Africa, and many parts of Asia, fear and power most likely rule a person's routine. This worldview emphasizes the middle, unseen world that exists between heaven and earth—the world of angels, demons, and magic. Some people and objects take on special powers and people live in bondage to those powers. Fear reigns both in the doing of certain things deemed wrong and the not doing of other things deemed right. For example, many people in these parts of the world are afraid to stop worshiping their idols for fear that something bad will happen to them.

The first time mankind experienced fear was when Adam and Eve hid from God in the garden.[12] Not only did they physically hide from God, they also tried to hide from his punishment by blaming someone else for their personal sins. Adam blamed the woman and the woman blamed the serpent.

---

[11] Genesis 3:6
[12] Genesis 3:8

Fear started by hiding from God and grew to blaming the spouse and serpent. Jesus dealt with this worldview frequently when displaying the power of God to heal people physically and spiritually, and perform other miracles. Jesus' signs showed everyone that the kingdom of God is near. When people witnessed the miracles of Jesus, they were released from the bondage of fear and empowered to experience God in a new way.

Shame and Honor. In places such as the Middle East, Korea, and Japan, shame and honor often control a person's daily life. Every action and reaction is filled with ramifications. Maintaining a good family name or reputation is the utmost priority. When a shameful act is committed, it is either covered up or avenged. Phrases such as "honor killing" and "saving face" make perfect sense to these communities.

Remember that God created Adam and the woman without clothing and without shame. Then, after eating the fruit, both the man and woman felt ashamed of being naked and used leaves to cover their bodies. Shortly afterwards, God replaced the leaves with animal skins. The skins came from the first blood sacrifice, in which an innocent animal had to die to cover the shame of man.

The gospel presentations that highlight the shame/honor worldview highlight the restoration of people's dignity. Examples from the Bible are the vindication of the woman caught in adultery in John 8 or Jesus' fellowship with the Samaritan woman in John 4. Issues of shame and honor are also essential to understanding the parable of the Son in the Field (commonly mislabeled as the Parable of the Prodigal Son) and Zacheus' encounter with Jesus. In the Old Testament the Hebrews lived in a shame/honor culture, so there are many Bible stories highlighting this concept. For example, the reason David fought Goliath was that Goliath was dishonoring the name of God. David was so upset that God's name was being ridiculed that he forgot about his size and felt compelled to restore the honor of God's name. In response, God honored David by giving him a victory and eventually making him king of the nation.[13] Both the Kingdom Analogy and the Eight Signs presentation (found in Chapter 3) are good places to start when addressing people in a shame/honor culture.

Other Worldview Issues. There is another facet that emerges from our study of death and its offspring, sin. It is a result of postmodern thinking and hinges on the question of purpose and meaning. Little children are not the only ones asking the question, "Why?" Instead, adults are wondering what really matters in life: What is a

---

[13] 1 Samuel 17

good life? What is a meaningful life? Who am I? The answer to the question, "Why?" must be God. Man has been placed on this earth to be an agent for God's work. Our purpose begins and ends in him, and he is the reason that the things we do and believe in have a purpose. Without him, there is nothing to live for.

Each culture makes up its own worldview regarding spiritual death and sin. Continue to learn how your friend understands the world and the personal experience of death. Is it related to a disease that took a young relative? Is it related to a never-ending chain of revenge in their home country? Is it a sense that all their daily prayers and fasting don't lead to a relationship with the God of love and mercy? Most people will be happy to answer questions when the questions come from a genuine heart. So ask questions and share Bible stories that fit the context.

Allow me to share a portion of a colleague's newsletter. This man does a wonderful job showing people what it means to live as a believer in the Middle East. In one of his notes he writes:

> When a Muslim Arab hears a quick synopsis of the gospel, something like, "Jesus died on the cross as a sacrifice for your sins, so you must believe in him to save you from your sins," what the hearer "heard" was probably not at all what was intended by the speaker. He

> most likely understood the speaker to be saying something like this: "Jesus, one of the most honored of the Apostles and Prophets of God, was slaughtered and defeated by the infidel Jews on a cross (the same cross that the Europeans wore when they came and slaughtered our people). So, I must believe in him (which I already do — I believe in all of the Prophets), and if I believe in Him, I can behave in any way I want without any accountability because I will be admitted to Paradise because they [Christians] believe that behavior isn't important, only beliefs. Now I understand why the Christian West is so immoral." Clearly something was missed in translation.

The gospel is the "good news," which is the message of forgiveness for sin through the atoning work of Jesus Christ. As you share this message, ask yourself how it can be communicated so that the hearer best understands it. The Holy Spirit will give wisdom within the moment, but that does not negate the importance of planning. When people understand their true standing before God, they will see the need for a Messiah.

The Person of Jesus, the Son Of God

Another point of discussion usually raised early in a spiritual conversation with Muslims is the

The Knowledge

person of Jesus and the title *Son of God*. Most Muslims recognize Jesus as one of the greatest people of all time. However, for the Christian, he is more than just a great prophet. He is the image of the invisible God, the first and last, the incarnation of the divine Word through whom the cosmos was created and so much more. Therefore, the main question becomes, "How do we talk to Muslims about Jesus without causing a fight or building a wall?"

Muslims respect Jesus and are convinced that they honor him better than many Christians do. The Qur'an treats Jesus with more respect and honor than it does any other person within the book. The Qur'an states that Jesus was sinless.[14] It also gives Jesus the title *Messiah* and records his virgin birth. However, within Islamic teaching there is no great significance assigned to any of these facts.[15] Even though there is a strong case for Jesus in the Qur'an, Muslims still follow Muhammad, the Prophet, instead of Jesus.

The Bible also states that Jesus was sinless, born of a virgin, and the Messiah. In the Bible we read many other things about Jesus and also why each one of them is significant. The people who met Jesus in person were confronted with a strong,

---

[14] Al Imran 3:46
[15] Maryam 19:19

confident man. He made claims to be one with his Father and to be Lord of the Sabbath. He accepted worship from others, knew what people were thinking, and healed people who were both physically and spiritual afflicted. Perhaps most poignantly, Jesus forgave sins—something that God alone can do. Each one of these signs points to his divinity.

Do you remember when the disciples were amazed after Jesus calmed the wind and waves in Mark 4? The disciples responded in awe, saying, "Who can this be, that even the wind and the sea obey Him!"[16] The disciples wrote about many events that left them speechless. Jesus set people free, restored them to the community, and lived his life as an example for everyone to follow.

From this brief discussion about the person of Jesus, we are able to make a plan for the way we will discuss Jesus with our Muslim friends. First, choose not to argue with people who have confrontation as their main agenda. Second, focus on what Jesus did and how he acted. In this case, it is not a problem to start with verses about Jesus in the Qur'an as long as you transition to the Bible at some point during the discussion.

If a Muslim states that Jesus never claimed to be God, point to passages where he did things

---

[16] Mark 4:41

equal to God. For example, he raised the dead, forgave sins, and accepted worship. Furthermore, if someone picks out a single Bible verse highlighting Jesus' humanity, read the entire passage and then consider the context. The Bible teaches that Jesus was fully God and fully man at the same time.[17] Therefore, share the full counsel of God in word and in deed.[18]

The Tri-Unity of God: Trinity

Often, it is difficult for Christians to talk about the Trinity. Admittedly, the doctrine itself is difficult to grasp, and many Christians know very little about the concept. Muslims typically believe Christians worship three separate gods. One of the reasons this is the case is because Christians are inaccurate in their use of the terms *Father, Son*, and *Holy Spirit*. To prove this point, listen to people pray in church. People will start praying to their Father and then start talking to Jesus, as if they were the same person! Printed books and sermons often are guilty of the same thing. Muslims end up confused and too often Christians are to blame. Jesus taught us to pray to our Father in heaven, so let us do that! If you wish, you may conclude your prayer by saying, "in the name of Jesus the

---

[17] Colossians 2:9
[18] Acts 2:27

Messiah" or "in the name of the one true God—Father, Son and Holy Spirit—Amen!"

In reality, without the revelation of the Trinity, mankind would not be able to grasp this interior dynamic of God's self-experience. Think about your own experience: What is it like for you to be you? How would you explain the richness of your own interior life to a being that is intelligent, but far, far inferior to you? For example, how would you explain yourself to an ant?

Islam claims to be a monotheistic religion, and Muslims are adamant that there is only one God. The Qur'an condemns a false trinity of God, Jesus, and Mary.[19] There has never been any documented church teaching like this, so it leads one to believe that Muhammad did not really know or understand Christianity.

When Muhammad was just starting out as a prophet, he witnessed people worshiping idols at the Ka'ba, the black cube-shaped building in Mecca. Initially, he preached against idol worship and polytheism. Most religions based on idols contain myths about gods in heaven mating with women on earth to bring forth demi-gods. Even though the Qur'an states that Jesus was born of a virgin, it is clear that Muhammad had no understanding at all of the meaning of the

---

[19] An Nisa 4:171

Christian doctrine of the incarnation. Likely, when he heard the talk of Jesus, Son of God, he associated this with the pagan stories he had heard about deities giving birth to other divine beings. Following this (misguided) logic, monotheism seemed to preclude any possibility of Allah having a son. By insisting God is alone, Islam limits God. In Islam, God is not omnipotent because, his Word cannot become flesh.

Let us now outline the biblical, orthodox, and historic doctrine of the Trinity. The Trinity is God's revelation to us of what it is like for God to be God. There are things humans can know about God apart from revelation, such as his power demonstrated in creation. The Trinity is not a doctrine invented by Christians. Rather, it is (I believe) something that God has shared with us about himself. This is a beautiful expression of God loving his creation by revealing himself so personally. It is also important to know what to *avoid* when talking about the Trinity. The main error that American Christians fall into is talking about parts. God is one God of one essence. Essences do not have parts—they are not like machines that can be taken apart or pizzas that can be divided. The divine essence of the increate Father is shared with the Son and the Spirit. The name of the relationality between the Father and the Son is called *generation* or *begottenness*. The name of the relationality between the Father and the Spirit is *procession*. The Son is eternally generated from the Father; the Spirit is eternally proceeding from the Father. Both of these relationships—generation and procession—are revealed to us in John's Gospel.[20]

If you don't know much about the doctrine of the Trinity, this is a great chance to grow in your knowledge of and relationship with God.[21]

Now that we have discussed the issue, commented on the Islamic teaching, and clarified the Christian doctrine, the question is how do we talk to Muslims about the Trinity in a clear and biblical manner that will make sense to them, or at least not build walls?

This is not a topic to raise early in a conversation, but it must be addressed eventually. Just as God revealed himself in the Bible via progressive revelation, it is best to build a foundation before discussing this topic with a

---

[20] For the Son, see John 1:18 and John 3:16; for the Spirit, see John 15:26.

[21] Peter Toon, *Our Triune God: A Biblical Portrayal of the Trinity* (Berkeley, CA: Regent, 1996).

Robert Letham, *The Holy Trinity: In Scripture, History, Theology, and Worship* (Phillipsburg, NJ: P&R, 2004).

Michael Reeves, *Delighting in the Trinity: An Introduction to the Christian Faith* (Downers Grove, IL: InterVarsity Press, 2012).

Muslim friend. If your Muslim friend insists on discussing it, take your time and emphasize that the Trinity is believed in the heart more than it is understood by the mind.

A devout believer, a convert from Islam to Christ himself, formally debated this topic several years ago and did a wonderful job. One of his main arguments was that there are many examples of the number three in our world. For example, time is measured in past, present, and future. Material is solid, liquid, or gas. Space is measured in height, width, and length. Based on this information, the debater made two points. First, he said the Creator has put his signature on all he has made. Second, since the principal of three-ness in one-ness, or trinity in unity, is very easy to comprehend in these cases (which cover every aspect of our world), why cannot God experience himself in the same way?

With this said, please know that illustrations like an egg, water, and the like probably do more harm than good. Instead, unlock the possibility of Trinity as it was done in the debate. In that debate, no one item from nature was said to be like God. Rather, the underlying principal in the created order of trinity in unity, or three-ness in one-ness, was emphasized. However, if you want to use an analogy from nature, the best one is probably that of the sun. The sun exists and from it come warmth and light. It is inconceivable to imagine the sun without it producing warmth and light. In the same way, the Son is eternally generated by the Father and the Spirit is eternally proceeding from the Father.

Finally, it is also possible to address this topic from a Qur'anic point of view. In the Qur'an, Jesus is called a *kalima* from God and a *ruuh* from God.[22] These are Arabic terms, the first meaning "a word from God" or "a word of God," and the second meaning "a spirit from God." God is not separated from his word nor his spirit, because they are both dynamics of who he is. God created the world through his word but he did not create his word. His word is always inherent in his being. The same argument is true for his spirit.

The doctrine of the Trinity is key to understanding the true God. When it is understood and handled properly, everyone benefits from an elevated understanding of who God truly is.

The Cross and the Atonement

Many Muslims ask, "If Jesus is God, how could God die on a cross?" or "Why would God allow Jesus, a highly honored prophet, to be killed in

---

[22] Al Imran 3:45, An Nisa 4:171 and Maryam 19:16-21

this way?" One of the biggest problems Muslims have with Jesus dying on the cross is that they believe it was a great defeat. However, Christians consider Jesus' death, burial, and resurrection the pivotal events in all of history. Consequently, they see the Crucifixion as a great victory. By dying once for all, Jesus restored the relationship between God and man, which had been damaged by sin.

Historically, there have been some Muslim scholars who agreed that Jesus did, in fact, die on the cross. However, the prevailing views that most Muslims champion are various mythical explanations about what "really" happened during the Crucifixion. For example: God made someone else look like Jesus, who died on the cross, and Jesus escaped; Jesus fainted but did not die; or, at the time of the earthquake, in the darkness, everyone ran away and Jesus climbed down from the cross unseen.

There are three verses in the Qur'an that mention the crucifixion and the death of Jesus. Maryam 19:33 is about Jesus, and it states, "And peace is on me the day I was born and the day I will die and the day I am raised alive." Some Muslims say this verse means Jesus will die someday in the future, but the original Arabic language does not support that idea. The second verse is Al Imran 3:55, which states:

> Behold! Allah said: O Jesus! I will take thee and raise thee to Myself and clear thee (of the falsehoods) of those who blaspheme; I will make those who follow thee superior to those who reject faith, to the Day of Resurrection: Then shall ye all return unto me, and I will judge between you of the matters wherein ye dispute.

The phrase, "I will take thee and raise thee to Myself," uses a key Arabic term, *mutawaffika*. The word is based on the verb *tawaffa*, which normally means "to pass away or die." In other Qu'ranic verses *tawaffa* is translated this way but oddly, not in 3:55. In other words, a logical reading of 3:55 is, "I will cause you to die, and [then] raise you up to me..." When looking at these two verses together, it seems that the Qur'an states that Jesus died and rose again. The third verse is An Nisa 4:157, which states:

> That they said (in boast), "We killed Christ Jesus the son of Mary, the Messenger of Allah," but they killed him not, nor crucified him, but so it was made to appear to them, and those who differ therein are full of doubts, with no (certain) knowledge, but only conjecture to follow, for of a surety they killed him not.

Technically, the Qur'an is correct on this point; the Jewish people did not kill Jesus. In reality, the Romans killed Jesus. Although Muslims point to this verse as their proof, it does not say that Jesus did not die on a cross. Instead, the only topic addressed by the verse is a claim made by Jewish people of that day, that they were not the ones who killed Jesus. When one reads the Qur'an within this type of logical framework, one must conclude that its author did not truly understand Christianity or Judaism.

For the Christian viewpoint, we will look at one portion of Scripture from the Old Testament and another from the New Testament. There are many verses and stories we could point to, but for the first example, let us focus on Isaiah 53:3-6.

> He was despised and rejected by mankind, a man of suffering, and familiar with pain. Like one from whom people hide their faces he was despised, and we held him in low esteem. Surely he took up our pain and bore our suffering, yet we considered him punished by God, stricken by him, and afflicted. But he was pierced for our transgressions, he was crushed for our iniquities; the punishment that brought us peace was on him, and by his wounds we are healed. We all, like sheep, have gone astray, each of us has turned to our own way; and the Lord has the laid on him the iniquity of us all.

This scripture is a prophecy about the Messiah, and each one of these individual statements was fulfilled in Jesus at his passion and death. Actually, Jesus fulfilled over three hundred Old Testament prophecies about the Messiah.[23] Even though evil men thought they were getting rid of Jesus forever, these men actually were fulfilling the prophecies of Isaiah. The punishment and shame that you and I deserve were put upon Jesus instead. This was the plan of God fulfilled in Jesus.[24] Because of the cross, you and I can gain a life of freedom and joy.

When using the New Testament to refer to Jesus' death and atonement, it is best to use passages that resonate with the Muslim mind. John 3:14 states, "And just as Moses lifted up the serpent in the wilderness, so must the Son of Man be lifted up." In this passage, Jesus compares his death with an event that is recorded in Numbers 21. In that story, the Children of Israel sinned and God sent poisonous snakes into their camp. Moses prayed and God instructed him to make a bronze snake and put it on a pole. Then, he told the people that the only way they could be saved was by looking to the pole in faith. In the same way, the

---

[23] Robert Saucy, *Scripture* (Nashville, TN: Word Publishing, 2001), 77.
[24] Graeme Goldsworthy, *According to Plan* (Downers Grove, Illinois: Intervarsity Press, 1991). An excellent overview of God's plan as found in Scripture.

only way you and I are saved is by looking to the cross in faith.

There are many ways to talk to your Muslim friends about the Crucifixion. However, it will take time for them to reach a point of belief. If you are talking about the historicity of the event, then there are four short arguments that make sense. First, the Roman soldiers were professional killers who crucified thousands of people during this period of history.[25] They knew how to kill someone and knew when that person was dead.

Second, Jesus predicted his death and led the way to Jerusalem. In Matthew 20:18-19 Jesus states:

> We are going up to Jerusalem, and the Son of Man will be delivered over to the chief priests and the teachers of the law. They will condemn him to death and will hand him over to the Gentiles to be mocked and flogged and crucified. On the third day he will be raised to life!

It is important to clarify that Jesus was not defeated or murdered on the cross. Instead, he willingly went to the cross on our behalf; he chose self-sacrifice. Jesus could have avoided going to Jerusalem and lived a long, peaceful life. Instead, we find Jesus making statements such as, "I lay

---

[25] John Stott, *Cross of Christ* (Downers Grove, Illinois: Intervarsity Press, 1986), 24.

down my life for the sheep,"[26] and "Therefore my Father loves me, because I lay down my life that I may take it again. No one takes it from me, but I lay it down of myself."[27]

Third, the sermons of Peter recorded in the book of Acts provide proof.[28] Each time Peter preached, he referenced the death, burial, resurrection, and ascension of Jesus. And every time, the crowd either remained silent or asked how they could be saved. Peter preached shortly after the events happened in the same city in which they had occurred. If these events had not taken place, the local people would have had a different response.

The fourth proof of the historical event comes from extra biblical authors of that day. Both Tacitus and Josephus are considered trustworthy sources, and both men mention that the crucifixion of Jesus was a historical fact.[29]

In short, each of the arguments that Muslims raise against the Crucifixion results in calling God a liar. The Old Testament prophets said the Messiah would die on a cross; Jesus predicted his death in advance; and then the New Testament

---

[26] John 10:15
[27] John 10:17-18
[28] Acts 2:23, 2:36, 3:14-15, 4:10, 5:30, 7:52
[29] http://www.josephus.org/quotes.htm. Accessed on September 23, 2016.

writers recorded the event. If God changed the appearance of Jesus during the event or if Jesus snuck away at one point, then the past two thousand years of Christian beliefs and teaching have been a lie. God is the God of truth, and if we cannot trust him in one thing, we cannot trust him in anything. People who deny the Crucifixion are making a serious claim against God and should be alerted to that fact.

Islam is correct in saying God cannot die. However, the story does not end with the death of Jesus. The Bible teaches that the physical body of Jesus died during the Crucifixion, but his soul, a union of the divine Word of God with the Father in heaven, remained alive. The Bible tells us that God is Spirit.[30] In other words, the *man* Jesus died on the cross, but *God* never died.

Jesus, being God, was the only one who was able to atone for the sins of man. He was the perfect God-man, taking the punishment for our sins while maintaining the perfection that is of God. It is one thing to say Jesus died on a cross, but it is another thing to say he died for us as individuals.

---

[30] John 4:24

One Gospel

A newer argument is that modern-day Christians do not follow the gospel of Jesus but rather the gospel of Paul. Few Muslims who make this claim are able to articulate it in any depth. However, sometimes people point to an isolated Bible verse or two to "prove" their point.

Drawing on the scholarship of some liberal Christian scholars, Muslims sometimes propose that Jesus simply taught a variation of Judaism. Later, Paul rejected his Jewish heritage and cast Jesus as the Son of God and God in the flesh—attributes which, according to them, Jesus never claimed to possess. We Christians, they say, don't really follow Jesus; rather we follow Paul.

The problem with this argument is that it presupposes some huge gulf between what Jesus really said and what Paul taught about him. It also implies that there was a true church founded by Jesus and a rival church established by Paul. But this does not fit well with Paul's own writings. Consider what Paul wrote in 1 Corinthians 1:22-25.

> Jews demand signs and Greeks look for wisdom, but we preach Christ crucified: a stumbling block to Jews and foolishness to Gentiles, but to those whom God has called, both Jews and Greeks, Christ the power of God and the wisdom of God. For the foolishness of God is wiser

than human wisdom, and the weakness of God is stronger than human strength.

This does not sound like someone who is changing the message of Jesus in order to get more followers. Paul complemented and revered the teaching of Jesus.

The verse that is used most often to summarize the gospel message is 1 Corinthians 15:1-5.

> Now, brothers and sisters, I want to remind you of the gospel I preached to you, which you received and on which you have taken your stand. By this gospel you are saved, if you hold firmly to the word I preached to you. Otherwise, you have believed in vain. For what I received I passed on to you as of first importance: that Christ died for our sins according to the Scriptures, that he was buried, that he was raised on the third day according to the Scriptures, and that he appeared to Cephas, and then to the Twelve.

Let me make a few points based on the verses above. First, Paul states that the Messiah died for our sins according to the Scriptures. This statement confirms the messianic prophecies of Psalm 22 and Isaiah 53. Added to this, when Jesus instituted the Lord's Supper in Matthew 26:28, he stated that his blood was poured out for the forgiveness of sins.[31] So, the first point Paul made is consistent with both the Old Testament and the teachings of Jesus. The second point, "He was buried," was prophesied in Isaiah 53:9 and fulfilled in Mark 15:46. The third point, "He rose again the third day according to the Scriptures," is also found in both the gospels and the teachings of Paul. The final statement that Paul made about the gospel is that the Messiah was seen after his death and burial. Although there is not one clear passage in the Old Testament that states Jesus will be seen on earth immediately after his resurrection (it does clearly say he will resurrect), Psalm 16 contains a passage that alludes to the fact. On the other hand, the four Gospels record many accounts of people seeing Jesus after he rose again. In Matthew 28, Jesus talks to women at the tomb; in Mark 16, Jesus appears to his disciples and to two other disciples on the road to Emmaus. His final appearance is at the ascension on the Mount of Olives when he was seen by over five hundred people, as recorded in 1 Corinthians 15:6.

The gospel message preached by Paul was consistent with the teachings of Jesus and with

---

[31] Simon Kistemaker, *New Testament Commentary 1 Corinthians* (Grand Rapids, MI: Baker Academic, 1993), 529

what was written throughout the Bible. If your Muslim friend tries to say that the teachings of Paul are different from the teachings of Jesus or the Old Testament, consider that to be an invitation for you to begin an in-depth Bible study with your friend. As was said in an earlier chapter, look for opportunities to join your Muslim friend on a faith journey.

SUMMARY

This chapter focuses on what a believer needs to know to be an effective witness among Muslims. The chapter opens with the premise that the worldview of most Muslims is influenced by: (1) a belief that everyone in the West is a Christian, (2) the fact that Islam is a community, and (3) a Muslim tendency to address four or five major topics all at one time. This was followed by the example of making chai. Remember, the point was that it is important to filter everything through the Bible.

Following this introductory information, the main section of the chapter highlights seven key areas that are frequently points of contention between Muslims and Christians. The seven categories are: the Holy Scriptures, God and Allah, Sin, the Person of Jesus, the Tri-Unity of God, the Crucifixion, and One Gospel. Each section opens with a statement of the issue, and then highlights the Islamic and Christian viewpoints before giving a series of practical responses. Knowing both the Islamic and Christian teachings is important.

When you are confident in your knowledge of Scripture and secure in your walk with God, you will naturally give a confident answer in love and peace. There is no reason to argue and fight with Muslims. The truth will stand on its own. As followers of Jesus, we have the truth and we have answers to the questions people ask. Therefore, pray for opportunities to share what God has revealed through his Word.

In short, our response to working with Muslims becomes fourfold. First, we are to pray; second, we must be servants; third, we must take every opportunity to introduce the culture of Jesus; and fourth, we must obey Jesus in every part of our lives. In Chapter 6, this discussion continues by showing that God is the only one who can stand in the gap between our sinfulness and his righteousness. No other substitute is worthy.

Chapter 6
THE TRUE RELIGION

In the previous chapter, I shared with you some information and insights that I have found to be important over years of cross-cultural ministry among Muslims. There, the focus was on knowing about Islam and being able to respond to some key questions that you will be asked, sooner or later.

But what about your own religion—Christianity? It is not only important to effectively address objections, but to provide an accurate portrayal of what you are inviting your Muslim friend to embrace and the community you are inviting them to enter. With that in mind, this chapter is born out of the conviction that there is something deeply flawed with the way most Americans understand the concept of religion. For instance, one hears statements such as, "Jesus didn't come to start a religion," or "Christianity is a relationship, not a religion." I understand that each of these statements is trying to make a valid point—that Christianity has a relational component that transcends and subsumes the ritual elements. But they are both inaccurate statements.

To say that Jesus didn't come to start a religion assumes that back in Jesus' day, there was something called *religion,* and that Jesus was aware of religion and wanted nothing to do with it. Historically, that is just not the case. There was indeed Judaism, which was an ethnic culture of people trying to live out a covenant with God. That is certainly not what is meant by the word *religion* today.

There were also many cults, and by this I mean sets of rules and rituals whereby a human or community could worship and thereby try to placate a deity, but these were not at all exclusive. For example, one could worship the local city goddess; then when his wife got pregnant he might give an offering to the goddess of fertility. Or a son might go to war and the parents could pray to the military god, and so on. One could participate in any number of these cults, which in themselves were tied up closely with the idea of citizenship. That is to say, if people did not participate in them, they were seen as traitors to their nation and people. Cultism is clearly not what people think of today as a religion.

Today's concept of religion did not exist in Jesus' time. To say that Jesus did not come to start a religion is like saying that Newton disagreed with the Theory of Relativity. He could neither agree nor disagree with that theory, as the concept itself had not even been formulated in his lifetime.

Let us consider the statement, "Christianity is a relationship, not a religion." I like this slogan a lot but not because I think it is true. (It is neither true nor untrue; it is nonsense—a misuse of words.) I like the slogan because it demonstrates in a coherent way how we American Christians have largely given up on serious, critical thought and embraced catchy jingles in their place. The problem with this statement is that it involves a false dichotomy: Christianity is *either* a religion, *or* it is a relationship. Why not both? Why not be a religious relationship, or a relational religion? The word *religion* comes from the Latin for "reconnect" or "reunite." And is that not precisely what Christianity claims to do—to reconnect, reunite, and reconcile people to their God? The cross and resurrection are the means whereby people are reconnected to God. Indeed, if Christianity were *not* able to reunite humans to God, only then, in truth, would it not be a religion at all.

So what *did* Jesus have in mind when he called us to him? To what are we inviting Muslims? Let's begin with the statement that Jesus clearly founded a community and a movement. What did he want to accomplish in founding this community, this body that is a "called out assembly" according to the meaning of the Greek word for church (*ekklesia*)? He gave us a leadership structure, a mission statement, a method for growth, a code of conduct, and rituals.

LEADERSHIP STRUCTURE

Jesus gave his community a leadership structure. There is no question that the apostles were given a great amount of authority—to forgive sins, to perform miracles, and so on. In Scripture, we see how they later used the laying on of hands (usually called ordination) in order to communicate and symbolize the transfer or sharing of that authority/vocation to other people whom they identified as being called by God.

MISSION STATEMENT

Jesus gave his community a clear mission statement. In Matthew, Mark, and Luke, Jesus is always talking about the kingdom of God, which, he says, is like a net, or someone sowing seeds, finding a hidden treasure, or owning a vineyard. Jesus' miracles and healings, likewise, are signs that the kingdom of God has come near. Jesus' favorite title for himself was *Son of Man*, which comes from Daniel 7, showing us an apocalyptic figure who receives eternal authority from God (the Ancient of Days, in Daniel) to rule not just over

Israel (as King David did), but over all the nations of the earth:

> As I watched in the night visions, I saw one like a human being coming with the clouds of heaven. And he came to the Ancient One and was presented before him. To him was given dominion and glory and kingship, that all peoples, nations, and languages should serve him. His dominion is an everlasting dominion that shall not pass away, and his kingship is one that shall never be destroyed (Daniel 7:13-14).

This is the gospel, or good news: that Jesus Christ right now is king over the entire universe; his kingdom has been established, and it is firmly grounded.[1] However, most of humanity is blind to this reality, and so Jesus founded a community (the church) in order to proclaim this gospel to all the peoples of earth: "And this good news of the kingdom will be proclaimed throughout the world, as a testimony to all the nations; and then the end will come" (Matthew 24:14). Before the final judgment and the righting of all wrongs, the nations must be given an opportunity to turn to God and receive forgiveness and reconciliation through Jesus Christ. And this is why Jesus

---

[1] The book to read on this topic is *The Gospel in a Pluralist Society* by Lesslie Newbigin (Grand Rapids: Eerdmans, 1989).

founded the church—in order to take this message of the kingdom to all the peoples of the world.

METHOD FOR GROWTH

Jesus gave his community a method for growth, having discerned that the church was to grow through discipleship. "Go into all the world, making disciples of all peoples..." Discipleship entails teaching by modeling, and we see this put into practice clearly when Jesus sends out the seventy-two (Luke 10) and then when Paul tells Timothy, "...and what you have heard from me through many witnesses entrust to faithful people who will be able to teach others as well" (2 Timothy 2:2).

CODE OF CONDUCT

Jesus gave his followers extensive instruction on ethics, which is to say, right and wrong. He talked about the right way of relating to money, family, the temple, the empire, the poor, and the ritually unclean. Indeed, the way that his disciples should live in the light of the kingdom of God constitutes the key part of his teaching in Matthew, Mark, and Luke.

RITUALS

Rituals are important to humans. Americans sometimes try to erase the significance of rituals, but they are deeply ingrained in us as human beings. Rituals are not something to run from but to embrace. I have heard people complain about "dead religion," which, as far as I can tell, refers to going through religious rituals and ceremonies without any emotional or spiritual connection to what is happening. The response to this is usually smoke machines, loud guitars, and drums, as if these somehow constitute a safeguard against spiritual death. But Jesus himself gave the church (at least) two rituals he wanted it to utilize on a regular basis: Baptism and Communion. They do not lead to dead religion at all, but to a lively and working religion called Christianity.

SUMMARY

Jesus himself founded the church—with a leadership structure, a mission, a method for growth, a code of conduct, and rituals. Once this assembly or church had grown significantly, it became clear to the ancient world that it was not the sort of thing that had ever existed before. It engaged in an exclusive worship (unlike the pagan cults) to one God, but it was not an ethnic God (how the God of the Jews was often perceived). This church gathered people from many languages and ethnic backgrounds and constituted them into a new people or nation not based on blood or language, but based on a common faith. What could the ancient world call this novelty? This is where we find religion starting to have the meaning we attach to it today. I would further note that the idea that religion can be completely separated from government is a fairly recent idea and largely limited to the post-Enlightenment West.

Returning to topic of whether or not Jesus founded a new religion, we should say, in summation, that Jesus founded a community (the church), and when the ancient world tried to find a word to describe this novelty, the best they could do was *religion.*

Now why is this lengthy discussion on religion in a book about Muslims in America? There is a method to my madness here. One of the main reasons is that Muslims do not have a flawed understanding of religion that most secular folks in the West do. They do not believe that religion needs to be hidden away in churches and homes. They do not believe that reason is attached to science, while faith (which is generally construed as being alienated from reason in the West) is attached to religion and that the two spheres do not overlap. Actually, Muslims tend to understand the concept of religion in the way that our medieval ancestors of Christendom did: that the reign of God can and should inform the governing of the city and the state. I believe that if we approach the Muslim with the secularized and unbiblical vision of religion so common in America today, it will be neither attractive nor intelligible to many of them.

In summary, Jesus founded the church, and the church is the visible community that points to the invisible but very real kingdom of God. The way of living and worshiping among Jesus' disciples in his church is called *Christianity*. It is to this way of life that we invite all Muslims. It is a way of living in relation to God and one another, which at times affirms the cultural customs of new members, while challenging others. Christianity itself is not a culture, but it is always challenging, forming, and reforming our own diverse cultures so that they will more and more reflect the invisible but powerful truth that right now, in all places, Jesus, the Son of Man, is Lord.

CONCLUSION

In this book, I started by making a case for a great need and then presented what I believe to be the correct perspective from which Christians in the United States should understand and think about our growing Muslim population. In Chapter 3, I outlined some practical ways that individual Christians can become better witnesses to their Muslim neighbors, and in Chapter 4, I outlined several ideas for whole churches that want to reach Muslims with the gospel of Jesus Christ. In Chapter 5, I presented some important information about Islam and apologetics, so that Christians who love their Muslim neighbors will be able to answer some standard questions that often surface. And finally, in the final chapter, I argued for a more robust and sturdy understanding of the meaning of the word *religion*—and that Christianity is the religion of the community founded by Jesus Christ himself, which he called the *church*. Rather than being embarrassed by these words (church, religion), we should rejoice in them, understanding them as strengths and not weaknesses as we share the good news.

It is my prayer that this book gives you ideas for practical ways for you and your church to form relationships with your Muslim neighbors. Because you love them and because your Father loves them, I hope you will share the gospel with them, inviting them to know the God and Father of our Lord Jesus Christ, and through the work of the Holy Spirit, join themselves to his body and bride, which is the church.

All around the world, there are men and women who grew up in Islam but later decided to leave Islam for Christ, his gospel, and his community of disciples. Rather than being filled with fear or anxiety or worry, be filled with power and love, knowing that with God all things are possible. One of those possibilities is that he would use you and your church to bring your Muslim neighbors to a living and firm faith in Jesus Christ.

Appendix 1

QUR'AN VERSES ABOUT THE HOLY BIBLE

Al Baqarah 2:41	Believe in the before scriptures.
Al Baqarah 2:53	Scripture was given to Musa (Moses) so the people could know the right way.
Al Baqarah 2:181	There is curse for any who change the Quran.
Al Imran 3:3	Both the Taurat and the Injil (some say gospels others say all NT) are revealed by Allah.
Al Imran 3:4	If you do not believe in the Taurat and Injil you will be severely punished.
Al Imran 3:78-79	Israelites teach and study scripture.
An Nisa 4:47	Believe in the Before Books that were given to you.
An Nisa 4:82	No contradictions in Bible.
An Nisa 4:163	Believe in ALL the before scriptures.
Al Maidah 5:41	Israelites possess the Scripture
Al Maidah 5:43	Taurat is a judge.
Al Maidah 5:46,48	Taurat is the command of Allah.
Al Maidah 5:68	"O People of the Book! Ye have no ground to stand upon unless ye stand fast by the Law, the Gospel, and all the revelation that has come to you from your Lord."
Al Maidah 5:69	Jews and Christians gain guidance only from Taurat and Injil
Yunnus 10:37	Confirms and explains Bible.
Yumans 10:64 (18:27)	Allah's words do not change.

Yunnus 10:94-95	If you have questions ask the people who have the before scriptures.
Al Isra 17:82 (36:5-10, 42:7)	Qur'an was revealed for Arabic speakers in Muhammed's time.
Ak Kahf 18:27	Allah's words don't change.
Fatir 35:31	Before Books are true.
Al Buruj 85:22	Bible called mother of all books.
Five Qur'an verses are sometimes used to "prove" the Bible is wrong. Each one says the teachers taught false things, not that the book was changed. They are 3:78, 2:75, 4:36, 5:13, 5:41.	

THE CLAIMS OF THE QUR'AN

The Qur'an states that the Holy Bible is:

Inspired by Allah	Nahl 16:43
Written by Allah	Anaam 6:91
Revealed by Allah	Shora 42:15; Al Imran 3:3
Confirmed by Allah	Hud 11:17
Given by Allah	Anaam 6:154; Isra 17:55; Al Maidiah 5:46
Preserved by Allah	Hijr 15:9; Al Maidiah 5:48

The Qur'an states that it:

Confirms/certifies the Holy Bible.	Fatir 35:31; Al Maidiah 5:46
Preserves the Holy Bible.	Al Maidiah 5:48
One should not reject what Allah has revealed in the Holy Bible.	Al Maidiah 5:44

Appendix 1

The Qur'an states that the Bible has:

Allah's commands	Anaam 6:115
Guidance and Light	Anaam 6:91
Leading and Mercy	Hud 11:17
Truth	Yunis 10:94-95

The Qur'an states that everyone:

Should believe in the Before Books.	An Nisa 4:136
Ask those who read the Holy Bible when they have questions or doubts.	Yunis 10:94-95
Believe in the Holy Bible.	An Nisa 4:136; Shora 42:15

THE CLAIMS OF THE BIBLE ACCORDING TO ISLAM

The Holy Bible states that it is:

Inspired by Allah	2 Timothy 3:16
Written by Allah	Hebrews 12:1-2
Revealed by Allah	Jeremiah 31:33; Romans 3:2
Confirmed by Allah	Matthew 5:17-18
Given by Allah	2 Samuel 23:2
Preserved by Allah	Psalm 119:89; Luke 21:33
Eternal	Luke 16:17; Luke 21:33

The Holy Bible:

Makes a person wise to salvation	2 Timothy 3:15
Is profitable for doctrine, reproof, correction and righteousness	2 Timothy 3:16
Equips a man for every good work	2 Timothy 3:17

The Holy Bible contains:

Allah's commands	Deuteronomy 5:5; Isaiah 2:3
Guidance and Light	Hebrews 4:12
Leading and Mercy	2 Peter 1:19
Enlightenment	Psalm 19:8; Psalm 119:130
Truth	Psalm 119:160

Appendix 2

QUR'AN VERSES ABOUT JESUS

1. HIS HUMAN POSITION	2. HIS SPECIFIC ROLES

He is Man
    Al Imran 3:59
    Al Maidah 5:116
    Saff 61:14
 	
Son of Mary
The Only One Called by His Mother's Name
    Al Maidah 5:114
    Al Maidah 5:75
 	
Righteous
    Al Imran 3:46
    Anam 6:85
 	
An Example
The only one called an example.
    Zukhruf 43:59
 	
A Slave
    Zukhruf 43:59
    Maryam 19:30
    An Nisa 4:172
	Prophet
	    Maryam 19:30
	
	Messenger
	    Al Maidah 5:75
	    Al Baqarah 2:253
	    Al Imran 3:49
	
	God's Messenger
	    An Nisa 4:171
	    An Nisa 4:157
	    An Imran 3:53
	
	Preferred
	    Al Baqarah 2:253

3. HIS EXALTED NAME	
Messiah (Christ) The only one called the Messiah (An Nisa 4:172, Al Maidah 5:72, Al Maidah 5:75).	**Heals** God and Jesus are the only ones who can heal (Al Imran 3:49).
A Miracle or Sign The only one called a sign (Anbiya 21:91, Maryam 19:21).	**Creates** God and Jesus are the only ones who can create (Al Imran 3:49).
Blessed The only one called blessed (Maryam 19:31.	**Gives life** God and Jesus are the only ones who give life (Al Imran 3:49).
Giver of Peace The only one to pronounce peace upon Himself (Maryam 19:33).	**Prophesizes** The only one who can prophesy (Al Imran 3:49).
Brought Near to God The only one who was brought near (Al Imran 3:45).	**Brings Forth the Dead** The only one who can raise the dead (Al Maidah 5:110).
Witness The only one said to be at the Day of Judgment Al (Maidah 5:11, An Nisa 4:159).	**Permits Forbidden Things** The only one who can do this (Al Imran 3:50).
Spirit The only one who is the Spirit of God (Anbiya 21:91, Talaq 66:12, An Nisa 4:171).	**Mercy** The only one called mercy (Maryam 19:21).
Aided by the Holy Spirit The only one aided by the Holy Spirit (Al Baqarah 2:87, Al Baqarah 2:253, Al Maidah 5:110).	**Highly Exalted** The only one who is Highly exalted (Al Imran 3:45).
Confirmer The only one called confirmer (Al Imran 3:50).	**Statement of Truth** The only one called a statement of truth (Maryam 19:34).
Sinless The only one who is sinless (Maryam 19:19).	**Word** The only one called the Word of Allah (Al Imran 3:39, Al Imran 3:45, An Nisa 4:171).

Appendix 3
INDEX OF QUR'AN VERSES

Passage	Page No.	Passage	Page No.
Al Baqarah 2:41	109,159	Al Maidah 5:44	160
Al Baqarah 2:53	159	Al Maidah 5:46	159,160(2)
Al Baqarah 2:75	110,160	Al Maidah 5:48	159,160(2)
Al Baqarah 2:87	164	Al Maidah 5:68	159
Al Baqarah 2:181	109,159	Al Maidah 5:69	159
Al Baqarah 2:253	163(2),164	Al Maidah 5:72	164
Al Imran 3:3	159,160	Al Maidah 5:75	163(2),164
Al Imran 3:3-4	109	Al Maidah 5:110	164(2)
Al Imran 3:4	159	Al Maidah 5:114	163
Al Imran 3:39	164	Al Maidah 5:116	163
Al Imran 3:45	132,164(3)	Anaam 6:85	163
Al Imran 3:46	125,163	Anaam 6:91	160,161
Al Imran 3:49	163,164(4)	Anaam 6:115	161
Al Imran 3:50	164(2)	Anaam 6:154	160
Al Imran 3:55	134(3)	Al Araf 7:188	110
Al Imran 3:59	163	Yunnus 10:37	159
Al Imran 3:78	110,160	Yunnus 10:64	109,160
Al Imran 3:78-79	159	Yunis 10:94-95	160,161(2)
An Nisa 4:46	110	Hud 11:17	160,161
An Nisa 4:47	159	Hijr 15:9	160
An Nisa 4:82	159	Nahl 16:43	160
An Nisa 4:136	161 (2)	Al Isra 17:55	160
An Nisa 4:157	135,163	Al Isra 17:82	160
An Nisa 4:159	164	Ak Kahf 18:27	160(2)
An Nisa 4:163	160	Maryam 19:16-21	132

Index of Qur'an Verses, Contd.

Passage	Page No.	Passage	Page No.
An Nisa 4:171	128,132,163,164(2)	Maryam 19:19	126,164
An Nisa 4:172	163,164	Maryam 19:30	163(2)
Al Maidah 5:5	90	Maryam 19:31	164
Al Maidah 5:41	159,160	Maryam 19:33	134,164
Al Maidah 5:43	159	Maryam 19:34	164
Anbiya 21:91	164(2)	Saff 61:14	163
Shora 42:15	160,161	Talaq 66:12	164
Zukhruf 43:59	163(2)	Al Buruj 85:22	160

Appendix 4
INDEX OF BIBLE VERSES

Passage	Page No.	Passage	Page No.
Genesis 3	120	Isaiah 38:19	6
Genesis 3:6	120	Isaiah 53	142
Genesis 3:8	121	Isaiah 53:3-6	135
Genesis 22	55	Isaiah 53:9	142
Exodus 3-4	44	Isaiah 55:11	51
Exodus 3:11	44	Jeremiah 31:33	161
Exodus 3:13	44	Daniel 4:34-35	69
Exodus 4:1	44	Daniel 7	150
Exodus 4:10	44	Daniel 7:13-14	151
Exodus 4:13	44	Matthew 5-7	71
Exodus 12:24-27	6	Matthew 5:17-18	161
Numbers 21	137	Matthew 5:20	71
Deuteronomy 5:5	162	Matthew 7:21	70
Deuteronomy 6:4-9	6	Matthew 10:32	71
1 Samuel 17	122	Matthew 9:37-38	17
2 Samuel 23:2	161	Matthew 12:25	10
Job 9:33	113	Matthew 13:52	70
Psalm 9:7-8	69	Matthew 15:11	115
Psalm 16	143	Matthew 20:18-19	138
Psalm 19:8	161	Matthew 23:37	10
Psalm 22	142	Matthew 24:14	151
Psalm 119:89	161	Matthew 26:28	142
Psalm 119:160	162	Matthew 28:19	6,25
Ecclesiastes 7:28	95	Mark 1:17	69
Isaiah 2:3	162	Mark 4	126
Isaiah 37:16	69	Mark 4:41	126
Mark 15:46	143	Acts 8	81

Index of Bible Verses, Contd.

Passage	Page No.	Passage	Page No.
Mark 16	143	Acts 9	45
Luke 2:49	10	Acts 9:2	101
Luke 10	152	Acts 10:9-48	45
Luke 10:1-9	64	Acts 10:15	45
Luke 10:6	64	Romans 1:14-16	7
Luke 10:25-37	46	Romans 3:2	161
Luke 15	15	Romans 6	118
Luke 16:17	161	Romans 10:9	71
Luke 16:19-31	13	Romans 10:14-15	34
Luke 19:10	9	1 Corinthians 1:22-25	141
Luke 21:33	161(2)	1 Corinthians 3:6	50
John 1:18	130	1 Corinthians 9:19-23	52,58,29,76
John 1:29	120	1 Corinthians 15:1-5	142
John 3:14	137	1 Corinthians 15:6	143
John 3:16	130	2 Corinthians 9:6	62
John 4	81,122	Ephesians 1:22-23	79
John 4:24	140	Colossians 2:9	127
John 4:34	10	Colossians 3:23	96
John 8	122	2 Timothy 1:7	44
John 10:15	138	2 Timothy 2:2	152
John 10:17-18	138	2 Timothy 3:15	161
John 15:26	130	2 Timothy 3:16	161(2)
Acts 2:23	138	2 Timothy 3:17	161
Acts 2:27	127	Hebrews 4:12	162
Acts 2:36	138	Hebrews 4:15	113
Acts 3-4	7	Hebrews 11:39-40	13
Acts 3:14-15	138	Hebrews 12:1-2	161
Acts 4:10	138	James 2:19	11
Acts 5:30	138	2 Peter 1:19	162
Acts 7:52	138		

Made in the USA
Middletown, DE
01 August 2017